THE FEW

THE FEW
A PHILOSOPHICAL DIALOGUE

Nicholas J. Pappas

Algora Publishing
New York

Library of Congress Cataloging-in-Publication Data

Names: Pappas, Nicholas J., author.
Title: The few : a philosophical dialogue / Nicholas J. Pappas.
Description: New York : Algora Publishing, [2024] | Summary: "In our modern
    democracies, in fact the people do not rule. Who does? This is a
    thoughtful, playful, yet serious exploration conducted by two friends
    who note that there are advantages to aristocracy as well as many
    drawbacks. The author shows that democrats can benefit from thoughtful
    consideration of their opposite model"— Provided by publisher.
Identifiers: LCCN 2024014861 (print) | LCCN 2024014862 (ebook) | ISBN
    9781628945362 (trade paperback) | ISBN 9781628945379 (hardcover) | ISBN
    9781628945386 (ebook)
Subjects: LCSH: Aristocracy (Social class) | Aristocracy (Political
    science) | Elite (Social sciences) | Democracy. | Imaginary
    conversations. | Dialogues.
Classification: LCC HT647 .P37 2024 (print) | LCC HT647 (ebook) | DDC
    305.5/2—dc23/eng/20240605
LC record available at https://lccn.loc.gov/2024014861
LC ebook record available at https://lccn.loc.gov/2024014862

Printed in the United States

More Books by Nick Pappas
from Algora Publishing

Controvert, or On the Lie and Other Philosophical Dialogues, 2008

Aristocrat, and The Community: Two Philosophical Dialogues, 2010

On Awareness: A Collection of Philosophical Dialogues, 2011

Belief and Integrity: Philosophical Dialogues, 2011

On Strength, 2012

On Freedom: A Philosophical Dialogue, 2014

On Life: Philosophical Dialogues, 2015

On Love: A Philosophical Dialogue, 2016

On Destiny: A Philosophical Dialogue, 2016

On Wisdom: A Philosophical Dialogue, 2017

All of Health: A Philosophical Dialogue, 2018

On Education: A Philosophical Dialogue, 2018

On Power: A Philosophical Dialogue, 2019

On Ideas: A Philosophical Dialogue, 2020

On Passivity: A Philosophical Dialogue, 2021

On Authority: A Philosophical Dialogue, 2021

On Violence: A Philosophical Dialogue, 2022

Looks: A Philosophical Dialogue, 2022

Rule: A Philosophical Dialogue, 2023

Comfort: A Philosophical Dialogue, 2023

PART ONE

SETTING: A CAMBRIDGE COFFEE HOUSE ON A FRIDAY, LATE AFTERNOON

* * *

1

Director: What time do you need to be home?

Lawyer: Mina took Bo up to the beach. I'm driving up tomorrow morning.

Director: Ah, you have all night. So tell me about work, and don't hold back.

Lawyer: Ha, ha. I still owe you a thanks for listening last week.

Director: No thanks needed. Well, what happened?

Lawyer: We won the trial.

Director: Congratulations!

Lawyer: Thank you.

Director: Now what?

Lawyer: Now I'm taking next week off.

Director: Time to soak up the sun and think. What will you think about? Your next case?

Lawyer: I like to think I have better things to think about than that.

Director: Such as?

Lawyer: Bo, for one. He's a teenager already. I can hardly believe it. I have so much catching up to do with him. We're going to fishing in the mornings, out on the water—if I can get him out of bed.

Director: Best to let sleeping dogs lie, but maybe not in this case. Fishing sounds nice. Do you ever catch anything?

Lawyer: Hardly. But Bo has luck.

Director: Good for him. And Mina, does she come?

Lawyer: She hates fishing. Also, she doesn't know how to swim. So she never goes out on the boat.

Director: That's too bad. What about the other lawyers who worked on the trial? Are they taking time off, too?

Lawyer: I insisted they do. It's one of the perks of being a partner.

Director: Yes, partners can insist. But tell me something, do you have an inner circle, a coterie?

Lawyer: I have people I like to work with, sure.

Director: And you have the power to reward them?

Lawyer: I have certain means within my discretion.

Director: Then they must love working with you.

Lawyer: I'd like to think they'd love working with me without the rewards.

Director: Yes, yes. But being part of the few always has rewards.

Lawyer: I'm not sure I like your grin.

Director: Just by being at your firm, you're part of the few. Being a partner at your firm makes you part of the fewer still. Being a regular winner makes you...

Lawyer: ...part of the inner sanctum. Ha, ha.

Director: But I'm not kidding. You're as inner circle as it gets.

Lawyer: And what do I have to show for it? I toil and toil long hours every day.

Director: You don't like what you do?

Lawyer: I guess I do. I mean, I must—right? Otherwise why do it? The money, sure. The prestige, yes. But money and prestige are never enough.

Director: You have to like what you do—or you're a fool. Yes, that's the bottom line.

Lawyer: Maybe I should say there are things about my job that I like. That's probably a better reflection of the truth. So maybe I'm a part-way fool.

Director: We're all part-way fools—the best of us, anyway. The few, the proud—the fools.

Lawyer: Do you think the aristocrats of ages gone by thought of themselves, in part, as fools?

Director: That's an interesting question. We have a tendency to think of aristocrats as eminently serious people. Maybe they weren't.

2

Lawyer: Yes, maybe. And maybe that humanizes them a bit. Aristocrats, through the lens of today, were somewhat... evil.

Director: Yes, evil. Precisely that. Except in romantic historical dramas, where they were—romantic.

Lawyer: Redeemed by romance, right.

Director: What's the problem with aristocrats, anyway?

Lawyer: They're not the equals of everyone else. They're not democrats.

Director: Ah, democrats. Are you a democrat, Lawyer?

Lawyer: I obey the laws, pay my taxes, and vote. That makes me a democrat, no?

Director: But what are you in your heart? Are you a democrat there?

Lawyer: Democracy is the worst form of government except for all the others.

Director: Sure. But do you really believe that? What about England at its aristocratic peak? Is that more to your taste? Or maybe France? Maybe you're more of a monarchist at heart.

Lawyer: I'm more of an aristocrat. I like having equals, my peers.

Director: But not everyone deserves to be your peer.

Lawyer: Do you think everyone deserves to be your peer? Or are you peerless, Director?

Director: Ha, ha. No, I don't think I'm peerless. My peers are philosophers.

Lawyer: Famous philosophers or any old philosopher?

Director: If it's a true philosopher? Any old philosopher will do. But I don't believe in an aristocracy of philosophers.

Lawyer: Are you saying philosophers can't be aristocrats?

Director: Francis Bacon was an aristocrat. Plato was an aristocrat. There are more who were. But they were philosophers despite that disadvantage.

Lawyer: Disadvantage? Ha! The two you named were probably as great as they were because they were aristocrats!

Director: Could be. But are you going to force me to go back to the pleb who started it all?

Lawyer: Socrates.

Director: Yes, Socrates. Was he a lover of aristocracy?

Lawyer: He couldn't have been.

Director: But he loved to spend time with aristocratic youth.

Lawyer: Time spent corrupting them, no doubt.

Director: No doubt. So what would you do with a Socrates today?

Lawyer: He'd have nothing to corrupt—no aristocratic youth.

Director: You don't think he'd seek out our few?

Lawyer: Few? What few? The few of virtue?

Director: What's wrong with virtue?

Lawyer: Ask your Socrates. He'll fill you in.

Director: Do you see something wrong with virtue?

Lawyer: Yes. I see it's in decline. Too many Socrates running around.

Director: I don't see that many Socrates running around. Do they hang out in top flight law firms? If so, please invite me in.

Lawyer: No, you're right. I'm thinking of people of the left in universities. They're no Socrates.

Director: What are they?

Lawyer: Resentful egalitarians.

Director: What do they resent?

Lawyer: The few.

Director: Why?

Lawyer: Because they don't belong.

3

Director: The resentful don't belong, or the few don't belong?

Lawyer: Both. The few are never resentful.

Director: They don't resent the resentful?

Lawyer: They despise the resentful.

Director: Maybe the resentful despise the few. But let's be clear. What kind of few are we talking about?

Lawyer: Those of excellence. Those of quality.

Director: Excellence of what? Quality of what?

Lawyer: It's hard to be precise. Let's just say you know it when you see it.

Director: What, is it how they carry themselves?

Lawyer: Yes, that's exactly it.

Director: And how do they carry themselves?

Lawyer: With dignity.

Director: Ah. So this isn't limited to a particular station in life. Even the most lowly can have dignity. But why limit it to dignity? Why not say the honest are few? That's true, isn't it?

Lawyer: True, the honest are few.

Director: And how about the wise? The wise are few, right?

Lawyer: It's the wise I have in mind. The wise are truly few.

Director: What are the wise wise in?

Lawyer: They have a certain understanding for how things work.

Director: How do things work?

Lawyer: Are you trying to get me to say I'm wise? I'm just saying the wise understand important things.

Director: The way government needs to function, for instance?

Lawyer: Yes, for instance.

Director: The way business needs to be conducted, for instance?

Lawyer: Yes, of course.

Director: The way people need to interact—manners and so on?

Lawyer: Definitely, yes.

Director: Hmm.

Lawyer: What is it?

Director: It seems to me we're talking about a ruling class.

Lawyer: Yes, but democracy has no such class.

Director: No legitimate ruling class, perhaps. And yet the few rule. Or don't you agree?

Lawyer: I do and I don't. Yes, the wealthy rule. But unlike a true aristocracy, they are forced to justify themselves to the many.

Director: And what's the problem with that?

Lawyer: It makes the whole thing a big charade!

Director: We all pretend the people rule, except for the people who know they don't rule.

Lawyer: Precisely.

Director: So if forced to choose between the grand charade and the rule of the people, which would you choose?

Lawyer: I honestly can't say. I hate the charade. And yet I do think the few should rule.

Director: You're not a democrat.

Lawyer: Of course I'm not a democrat. Are you? And don't tell me democracy is the worst form of government except for all the others.

Director: What if it is?

Lawyer: Then the few should drop the charade and embrace democracy.

Director: But isn't that what they say they do within the charade? You want them to embrace democracy wholeheartedly? But what if it's simply not in their hearts?

4

Lawyer: This will always be the problem for those of ability in a democracy. Yes, we all have some talent. But I'm talking about the ones with real talent. When they are told we're all equal before the law, yes, they completely agree that this is how it should be. But....

Director: But some democrats don't think that's enough?

Lawyer: No, they think we should be absolutely equal. Equal in all things. The ones with real ability don't understand how that's fair. And seeds of discontent are sown in their hearts.

Director: And what of people of real ability in a hereditary aristocracy? Suppose someone isn't born to the ruling class. Will their ability be recognized?

Lawyer: Those who rule choose lieutenants of ability. There is a path to rise.

Director: But what if the one outside the ruling class has more ability than that of a lieutenant? What if they have the ability of a king or queen?

Lawyer: Nothing is completely fair. But I'll be the first to admit—democracy might be better for them. They might be elected to preside.

Director: So would-be kings and queens prefer democracy to aristocracy. And that holds even when they're born into the ruling class—because aristocrats would never let them become the sole head of state.

Lawyer: This is a problem with aristocrats. They are very jealous of their power. If someone grows too strong, they team up to bring them down.

Director: Is it fair to say you're a supporter of the few over the one?

Lawyer: It is. One with great power is more dangerous than a few with that same amount of power divided up. To go with the few is to play it safe.

Director: And to go with the many?

Lawyer: That might be safest of all. But it reduces things to the lowest common denominator. An aristocracy allows nobler growths to thrive.

Director: Listen to you. I thought you would have said the risk of mob rule is great. How do we fight that risk?

Lawyer: We fight it by not having direct democracy. We are a representative democracy. That puts the brakes on things.

Director: And we also have a sort of watered down aristocracy in the Senate, right?

Lawyer: Right, and it's obvious what the executive branch is. But what do you make of the Court?

Director: Terms for life. The very few, yes?

Lawyer: Very few, yes. Imagine if we got aristocrats at heart onto the Court.

Director: They'd have to sneak their way on. People wouldn't stand for it if they knew.

Lawyer: That's true. But I worry about what the sneakiness does to the soul. What honor is there in that?

Director: There is no honor when you go sneaking around.

Lawyer: That's exactly the point. If you're sneaky on your way in, what's to say you won't be sneaky while you're there?

Director: Do you think aristocrats have more honor than the people?

Lawyer: Not necessarily. There can be very great honor among the people.

Director: And virtue? More among aristocrats?

Lawyer: This is a difficult question. If virtue means ability, then yes. If virtue means a kind of moral phenomenon, then no.

Director: Are we talking about hereditary aristocracies? Aristocracies of the blood? Is ability transmitted by blood?

Lawyer: Not always, but often enough.

Director: What proof do you have for your often enough?

Lawyer: People inherit traits. What can I say?

Director: But not always.

Lawyer: No, not always. Nothing is always.

Director: Isn't the selection by election of those with certain traits more reliable than transmission by blood?

Lawyer: It would be but for one thing. The democratic electorate avoids voting for those with aristocratic traits.

5

Director: What if aristocrats at heart did the choosing?

Lawyer: And those they choose become aristocrats for life? Here's the problem with that. True aristocrats are raised from birth to rule. What would you have us do? Raise every one to rule then select only a few? What kind of trouble does that engender?

Director: I think something like that happens in democracy. All are meant to have equal opportunity. This includes the opportunity to rule. But only certain people come to rule, whether in politics or business or whatever. Same sort of thing?

Lawyer: Here's the thing. The people you're talking about work for their rule, mostly. Aristocrats don't believe in work. They believe in cultivated leisure. That's what makes them hated by the many, who can never hope for as much.

Director: Why value leisure?

Lawyer: Why value the sweetest thing in life?

Director: All you need is free time in order to really live?

Lawyer: It takes something more. Rule. Rule is hard. It makes great demands on the soul. Rulers need lots of time to recover so they're prepared to rule when they must.

Director: So rule is their purpose in life? Everything leads up to that? Or is it rule for the sake of something else?

Lawyer: Rule is a duty imposed by necessity. At times necessity is sweet. But is rule the highest thing in life? I guess I've never thought of it that way before.

Director: What if it's rule for the sake of fame?

Lawyer: Those who discharge their duties well deserve to be famous, yes.

Director: So fame is the highest thing.

Lawyer: But you know that's not something peculiar to aristocracies. Kings want to be famous for being great rulers. Democrats claw one another for fame.

Director: Is fame everyone's highest thing? Is it for you?

Lawyer: Is it for you?

Director: Let me ask you this. Do the ambitious always long for fame? If so, we can say the highest thing for the ambitious is fame. Then it's a question of determining who is ambitious.

Lawyer: I don't know. I might have an ambition to make lots of money. Do I care if fame comes along with it?

Director: The rich are known for being rich. To be known is cousin to fame. No?

Lawyer: Alright. You have a point there. But what about someone who has an ambition to found and manage an animal shelter? Suppose they succeed? Famous?

Director: Within certain circles, sure. But I take your point. Their point wasn't fame. It was to achieve a certain thing. The fame might not even be an afterthought. And I can see how it might be that way with the rich concerning money. But what about those with ambition to rule? Is fame always linked to that?

Lawyer: Hold on. You've got me thinking. What is money but the ability to rule? Money makes others do what you want.

Director: Well, that's the dream concerning money. It doesn't always work.

Lawyer: No, but ninety-nine percent of the time it does. So the question is does rule, however achieved, point to fame.

Director: You can't rule for the sake of rule alone? What if someone really likes to rule, loves to rule? Who cares about fame? Only let me rule!

Lawyer: Ha! You make a good point. Maybe fame ensures there is virtue in rule.

Director: Do you mean that as ability or moral phenomenon?

Lawyer: Moral phenomenon. Raw ability can just as easily win you infamy as fame.

Director: Infamy might be harder to win.

Lawyer: What nonsense is this? You'd better explain.

Director: I said it might be harder to win. When is it harder? When everyone is virtuous. You're cutting against the grain.

Lawyer: Hmm. So honorable fame is harder to win when you're cutting against the grain of decadence?

Director: That makes sense to me. But then I'm not sure about the remaining cases. Honorable fame in honorable times; infamy in decadent times.

6

Lawyer: Honorable fame is always very hard to win. Infamy is always easy to win. That's what I think we have to conclude.

Director: Alright—though I think we might be doing an injustice to infamy.

Lawyer: The infamous deserve whatever injustice they get.

Director: That's funny. I like to think of justice as getting what you deserve.

Lawyer: Then the infamous get full justice when they get injustice from us.

Director: I'll have to think about that. It has something to do with telling the full story.

Lawyer: What's to tell with the infamous? They took shortcuts. That's the full story.

Director: That may be. Still, the infamous are few. Aren't they?

Lawyer: There are more than you might think—because their fame doesn't last long, in most cases.

Director: Good bye, good riddance, and then forgotten?

Lawyer: Yes, exactly that. It takes a real monster to win lasting fame.

Director: Why do you think people remember the monsters? It is just because they make such a lasting impression?

Lawyer: Yes, there's that. But I think it's because people don't want to forget—to ensure it never happens again.

Director: They want to nip the monsters in the bud.

Lawyer: They do. And they're often successful in this.

Director: How can we recognize incipient monsters?

Lawyer: You mean if they've yet to do anything monstrous? We curb all bad behavior, however mild. Latent monsters won't take to this well. They'll rebel against even the gentlest curb.

Director: So no independent spirits.

Lawyer: You know that's not what I mean. You can be independent—but within the rules, the rules of good behavior. In fact, independence is one of the good behaviors we teach.

Director: Monsters are dependent?

Lawyer: It's funny you should ask. I think it's true. Monsters are weak, dependent, probably clingy as youths. They're probably also spoiled. They grow up to be great big babies who cry when they don't get their way.

Director: And if they don't get their way often enough? They grow monstrous in their feelings inside. The outer behavior follows suit. Is that it? Is that our portrait of the monster?

Lawyer: I think it's an accurate portrait in many cases, though I don't doubt there are other paths to monstrosity.

Director: How does an aristocracy react to a monster among its ranks?

Lawyer: It does all it can do to keep power from his hands.

Director: He'll try to play you off each other.

Lawyer: Yes, no doubt he will. It's a real problem if he's as able as his blood would suggest.

Director: Why is it a real problem? The other aristocrats have good blood.

Lawyer: Yes, but you know the downside to aristocracy. Aristocrats are jealous of one another. A monster knows that and can play them here.

Director: Jealous for fame? Is that what they're jealous of?

Lawyer: In the end, yes. But they are also jealous of looks, money, titles, and so on.

Director: So there will be factions for the monster to exploit. How do factions play out in democracies?

Lawyer: Some of them band together out of expediency and claim to be the champions of the people. Others respond by banding together and claiming to be supporters of excellence and business rights. Things like that.

Director: Would an aristocracy always side with the latter because of their support of excellence?

Lawyer: Naturally. Aristocracies rarely side with the people.

7

Director: What about top flight law firms? Where do their sympathies lie?

Lawyer: It depends on the factions within. But it's usually best not to commit to one side or the other. It's too much of a risk, though there are some firms that do it. Always remember, these lawyers side with themselves, not others.

Director: Just as aristocrats side with themselves, not others. How about democrats? Do they side with themselves, not others? And what about kings and queens?

Lawyer: It's human nature for like to side with like.

Director: So monsters will side with monsters, whether they are aristocratic, democratic, or kingly monsters.

Lawyer: True, up to a point. Once they get what they want, they turn on those like them. They then seek to surround themselves with lackeys.

Director: Who does a successful aristocrat, one who's got what he wants, surround himself with?

Lawyer: If he's full of virtue? Other successful aristocrats. Those who have what they want. It's good to be around those who have what they want. They want nothing from you.

Director: So a successful aristocrat wouldn't surround himself with democrats, for instance.

Lawyer: True. They'd envy him. No matter their success, they'll never have his rank. And that burns.

Director: Is that why aristocrats make such wonderful patrons? They're never jealous of the artist commoners they support.

Lawyer: It's interesting to compare the masterworks of the aristocratic past to the products of the democratic age. All art today must appeal to the many. Art that doesn't is kept private or in small circulation at best.

Director: What's wrong with appealing to the many? Isn't that the benchmark of success? Having many delight and approve?

Lawyer: Which would you rather have? A thousand semi-literate people clamor that your book is great? Or a dozen refined readers say that it's really good?

Director: Fortunately, I have no published books so I don't have an opinion on this matter. But I must admit, winning praise from those who know is best.

Lawyer: You value the judgment of the few. That makes you, at heart, an aristocrat.

Director: But I'd value the judgment of the many if they knew. Knowledge is the thing. And I'm not persuaded that aristocrats are knowledgeable in all things.

Lawyer: Who is more likely to gain knowledge, refined knowledge? Someone who has to work sixty hours a week or someone with cultivated leisure?

Director: Aristocrats used to love spending their time in the hunt. Does that make them good judges of books?

Lawyer: They spent their early mornings in the hunt, their days in government, and their evenings with books. Doesn't that appeal?

Director: I confess. That does appeal. But here's how I spend my time. In the early morning I go to the gym. I then spend my day at work. And in the evening I read very good books. Am I an aristocrat of sorts?

Lawyer: The question is how you spend your day. Aristocrats rule in the broad light of day. Do you?

Director: I manage a team. Is that akin to rule?

Lawyer: Yes, but someone manages you. Aristocrats have no manager over them. They are equals with their peers. Yes, some have more authority is one area, others in another. But there is no manager to tell them what to do. They are free. Wouldn't you like to be free?

Director: I would. But I wouldn't like to spend all my time trying to protect that freedom, which is what I think aristocrats must do. It defeats the purpose.

Lawyer: You think they're not free?

Director: I think they're trapped.

8

Lawyer: And it's so much better to be a democrat, struggling to make ends meet.

Director: Don't you know of impoverished aristocrats who struggle to make ends meet?

Lawyer: That's because their aristocracies collapsed.

Director: Oh, I don't know. I think there have been poor aristocrats in every age. Do you know why that is?

Lawyer: Tell me.

Director: They didn't have the killer instinct to keep themselves in money.

Lawyer: Say more about this instinct.

Director: It's an instinct that, when push comes to shove, sides with gain. And push often comes to shove.

Lawyer: You earn a fair amount of money, don't you?

Director: I do. But I don't always side with gain.

Lawyer: What do you side with? Humanity? The truth? What?

Director: I side with my friends.

Lawyer: Ha, ha. I can see that in you. What about me? Where do I come down?

Director: You? You always side with the law. And we see what good that does you.

Lawyer: Ha! Plenty of good. If I had to guess I'd say I make around ten times what you make. Siding with the law pays.

Director: I never said it didn't. But you are persuasive in getting people to believe your view of the law is best. The law is funny. It admits of different views. I guess that's why we have the ultimate few, the Supreme Court nine. They rule the law but should be democrats at heart.

Lawyer: And if they're not?

Director: Well, they were appointed by the President and approved by the Senate. So either those two branches of government didn't know the justices weren't democratic, or they did know and approved them nonetheless.

Lawyer: Meaning the President and Senate aren't democrats at heart.

Director: That's what this seems to mean. Imagine if the Court were dominated by aristocrats at heart. Imagine if they took an aristocratic view of the law and ruled on this view. What would happen here?

Lawyer: Things would be looking up!

Director: Yes, things would be good for the few. In our case the few are the rich. I would count you among the rich. I would count myself among the well-to-do. Maybe the upper middle class? I don't know.

Lawyer: What's good for the rich is good for you, Director.

Director: You speak of the rich as if it were a class. But don't you look down on people who have to work like dogs to make themselves rich?

Lawyer: I work hard, you know.

Director: Do you? Hard? I know you work long hours—because you bill all those hours at outrageous rates. But are you working hard?

Lawyer: What else do you call it when you exhaust yourself in your work?

Director: Alright, you've persuaded me. You look tired today even though yesterday you won. I can only imagine what you looked like earlier in the week. But be honest. There are ways of making money that you look down on, aren't there?

Lawyer: There are.

Director: You don't want to be classed with these people, do you?

Lawyer: I don't. I want to be classed with the highly educated rich.

Director: What about the highly educated simply?

Lawyer: They are often rabid democrats at heart.

9

Director: Is there something about becoming rich that makes you lose your democratic heart?

Lawyer: Oh, don't be Charles Dickens here. We have to ask ourselves. What is a democratic heart? What does it mean to love people indiscriminately?

Director: What does it mean?

Lawyer: It means you're not making the effort to see people for what they are.

Director: You mean they're not all the same. But do you mean the few are different and the many are the same?

Lawyer: The few differ from the many. And yes, maybe the few are all the same; and the many are as varied as can be.

Director: What might make the few the same?

Lawyer: Virtue.

Director: The Marines had a marketing campaign in which they described themselves as the Few, the Proud. Do you admit the Marines to your few? They have virtue, after all.

Lawyer: If you bring me a highly educated, wealthy Marine, I would welcome him or her into the club.

Director: What is it about education, high education?

Lawyer: The few must be refined. The way to refinement is through education. High just means advanced. It means you have learned to work your mind, a skill not everyone has.

Director: But why the money? Why not just virtue and thought?

Lawyer: Money shows you have skin in the game. You have something at stake.

Director: I thought living free was what was at stake. Leisure.

Lawyer: Money, virtue, education, leisure. Without these things you can't be part of the few.

Director: It's a small class that you describe.

Lawyer: That's why we call it few.

Director: So I'm trying to imagine who belongs in this class. I don't. You don't.

Lawyer: I don't?

Director: Are you that forgetful, Lawyer? What leisure have you got? I know you're going on vacation starting tomorrow, but really! You're back to the grindstone soon. Or are you hinting that work isn't so much work for you? Maybe your work is like the ruling work of aristocrats of old? I know you. You play squash in the early morning. You work/rule all day. Then at night you love to read philosophers of old—when you're not out in society.

Lawyer: It's true. My work is like the rule of old. But it's only like it. Things could be much better.

Director: I'm sure they could. But how?

Lawyer: If I worked with my equals with no one above. As it is now, I have to answer to my clients.

Director: Maybe your clients are the aristocrats and you're their lieutenant? Ah, I see you don't like to look at it that way.

Lawyer: Ideally, my clients are my equals and I am helping them with their affairs.

Director: And if equals, maybe they don't pay you in cash? Maybe they owe you a favor?

Lawyer: Yes, something like that. We should stand on equal footing. Already, it's like that with many of those I work with. Yes, they pay me. But we look each other in the eye. That's what I want. Equality.

Director: The equality of the few. And what of the many?

Lawyer: Other sorts of lawyers can service them. Law is something I practice; it's not who I am.

10

Director: Who are you?

Lawyer: A member of my family.

Director: Ah, the family. People always speak of aristocratic families. The family is key. But isn't the family always key no matter the regime?

Lawyer: Yes, but in aristocracies the best families come to rule.

Director: How do they come to rule? Or is this one of those things better left unsaid, better to let your imagination wander down through the years to a golden age where the best were chosen and installed in rule?

Lawyer: Yes, if you want my honest opinion—that is best. No beginnings are perfect. But if we can make a good start, run with it I say.

Director: So a touch of mythology is good, maybe even is necessary.

Lawyer: That is my considered opinion.

Director: So the aristocrats might not be the absolute best.

Lawyer: Of course not. But if they're eighty percent the best, is that so bad?

Director: Eighty percent is pretty good. But how can we improve the rate of success?

Lawyer: We kick the bad ones out.

Director: Is that under extreme situations? I assume it's not a casual thing.

Lawyer: Hardly. But you know what goes with this. We bring the excellent in.

Director: How? Is there some sort of formal process?

Lawyer: There should be, yes. And it gives the people some hope that one day they might admitted to the ruling class. Just a little hope goes a very long way.

Director: Spoken like a true hereditary ruler. But the newly admitted must be of sterling character. There's not much room to mythologize with contemporaries.

Lawyer: Oh, you might be surprised. We wouldn't be looking for famous people. We'd want people of quiet virtue.

Director: You don't want anyone who will rock the boat.

Lawyer: We want people who will help sail the ship. And the first step in that is knowing what kind of ship you're on.

Director: But really, Lawyer, who doesn't know what kind of boat they're in?

Lawyer: Again, you might be surprised. We're looking for people who have a knowledge of sailing from earliest youth. We want people who can look at a ship and straight off say what kind it is, what it takes to sail it, what are its strengths and weaknesses.

Director: What's the strength of an aristocratic ship of state?

Lawyer: It moves beautifully in the water. It's a pleasure to see.

Director: And the weakness?

Lawyer: It's not as sturdy as a democratic regime. Or, I should say, it's not as sturdy as a properly tempered democratic regime. Otherwise you have a mob. Mobs always sink the ship.

Director: Is there a mob in America today?

Lawyer: There might be. With a bad enough economic turn? Some other sort of disaster? Who knows? But I'll tell you what's more likely. America will last another thousand years. All the signs are there.

Director: So you don't seriously hope for an aristocracy here.

Lawyer: Not as the law of the land, no. But pockets of aristocracy can exist within a democratic state.

Director: Why would the democracy allow such a thing?

Lawyer: Because it's preoccupied with other more pressing problems.

Director: So, and forgive me, you want there to be trouble.

Lawyer: I'm only telling you the truth. Democrats would hate me for this. And they already do because they intuit what's to my advantage.

Director: But can't the democrats sympathize? Doesn't everyone want leisure?

Lawyer: No, not everyone does. People don't know what to do with it. They get antsy, bored. They're at an utter loss.

Director: They don't know about ambitious leisure, like you.

Lawyer: My ambition is to cultivate myself, to make myself a beautiful human being.

Director: You really don't think many democrats want that, too?

Lawyer: Some do, yes. But many? Really? Is that what you believe? It's the best of the democrats who do. The rest drink beer and watch football with their time.

Director: I drink beer and watch football.

Lawyer: Oh, you know what I mean. You also read philosophy.

Director: I also read detective stories.

Lawyer: Are you trying to tell me you're a democrat at heart?

Director: No.

11

Lawyer: What are you at heart?

Director: A philosopher. But you knew that before you asked.

Lawyer: I'm just making sure.

Director: Are philosophers of use in aristocracies?

Lawyer: Why do you even have to ask! Of course! Philosophers are deeply concerned with the beautiful, as are all true aristocrats. We share a love for human excellence.

Director: And what of the many, as opposed to the few, who have a love for human excellence?

Lawyer: They'll get to witness excellent rule every day of their lives. And there's no reason why they can't consort with philosophers and do other things to cultivate themselves.

Director: How about literature? Will everyone be allowed to read?

Lawyer: I can't tell if you're being ironic. Sure, everyone will read. But I think your real question is whether there will be censorship. The answer is yes.

Director: What kind of censorship? Anything critical of aristocracy? Anything promoting democracy or some other form of rule?

Lawyer: Yes, all that—and anything crass. We want a beautiful society, not one made ugly by what it reads.

Director: So you don't believe in a marketplace of ideas.

Lawyer: No, I believe certain ideas are inherently better than others. Those are the ones to tout; the others should be hidden from view.

Director: But the censors will read them. You'll have to keep close watch on the censors. Not only might they be corrupted by their role, but they might be exposed to demand for a black market for books.

Lawyer: Once a good regime is in place, it won't be that hard to manage all these things.

Director: I suppose you'll come down with terrible harshness for the slightest offense.

Lawyer: You're right in your supposition. If aristocrats know one thing, they know where they need to be absolutely firm, unshakeable. They make no exceptions and make no mistakes, whether out of pity or whatever weakness might move them.

Director: That sounds a bit like a totalitarian regime. What's the difference?

Lawyer: Totalitarian regimes have no sense of beauty.

Director: That's it? Beauty saves the day?

Lawyer: Tell me something, Director. Would you be willing to live a life in which there were no beauty?

Director: No beauty at all? What kind of life would that be?

Lawyer: Exactly my point. Aristocracy is the only regime dedicated to beauty.

Director: The beauty of wonderful rule. The beautiful state.

Lawyer: Yes.

Director: What's your favorite aristocracy?

Lawyer: Well, England always comes to mind.

Director: Why? Wasn't that a balanced sort of regime? There was a king; there was a commons.

Lawyer: Maybe we have to look further back to Thucydides' ultimate regime— Sparta.

Director: That regime was dedicated to war. Is that what your modern regime would be? A warrior state?

Lawyer: That's not what I had in mind. But maybe I should.

Director: Your aristocrats can't be effete, can they?

Lawyer: Certainly not. They must command.

Director: Command the superior soldiers of the many?

Lawyer: No, they must be superior themselves.

Director: So it's not just moral qualities you seek. You're looking for perfect physical specimens.

Lawyer: I am.

12

Director: Then you have another dilemma.

Lawyer: What dilemma is that?

Director: If things with science keep on going the way they are, you might be able to engineer your perfect physical warriors.

Lawyer: Science....

Director: You don't like science?

Lawyer: Science knows no shame.

Director: You would teach science shame?

Lawyer: I absolutely would. But what's the dilemma? We'll make use of science, yes. We'll create the perfect fighting caste.

Director: But don't you want the many to be as strong as they can be, so that when you fight together you conquer?

Lawyer: You're thinking they might rival the aristocrats? Never. Physical form is one thing; ability to rule is another. Our aristocrats will learn rule from the cradle.

Director: And if a natural ruler arises among the plebs?

Lawyer: We cut them down. Are you surprised at my honesty?

Director: A little. But I know you must mean you cut them down to size. But I wonder. Is war the thing that keeps the aristocrats from growing corrupt?

Lawyer: War and early training, yes. Relax either of these things and it's all over. That's what I mean when I say aristocracies are fragile.

Director: Fragile yet cruel. Perhaps they're cruel because fragile?

Lawyer: You're no stranger to deep psychology. I admit the truth in that.

Director: Science isn't fragile, is it?

Lawyer: No, it's not.

Director: Democracy isn't fragile, is it?

Lawyer: No, despite all of the democratic propaganda that would make it seem so.

Director: Why would democrats want to appear fragile?

Lawyer: To garner sympathy.

Director: But why not be the bull frog and puff yourself up? Isn't that a good defense?

Lawyer: But who are they defending themselves against? Themselves.

Director: I don't understand.

Lawyer: If democrats believe there is a sort of inevitability in democracy, what reason do they have to try?

Director: Try to do what?

Lawyer: Excel. They need to flatter themselves in order to stir themselves to action. Poor old democracy is weak. It needs heroes in order to sustain itself. You know how it goes.

Director: I see. Always the underdog, this democracy.

Lawyer: Always the underdog, sure. Aristocrats don't think of themselves as underdogs. That's why it's easy for democrats to vilify them. And this is good for democracy.

Director: How so?

Lawyer: Democrats have a profound psychological need to cast themselves against overdogs.

Director: But what aristocratic overdogs are there in the world today?

Lawyer: A good question.

Director: So what do democrats do?

Lawyer: They focus on increasing equality wherever they can—equality in everything you can imagine.

Director: Why is this bad?

Lawyer: Because it goes against nature! Certain people are more equal than others.

Director: Certain people are better than others, you mean.

Lawyer: It's true. Aristocrats are better than the people. I know this sounds like the ultimate blasphemy, but there it is.

13

Director: You're basically saying they're more beautiful—in body, mind, and soul.

Lawyer: Yes. It's hard for us to believe this is possible. We've never seen a thriving aristocracy up close.

Director: Then how do you know it's possible?

Lawyer: I've been around the world many times over. I've seen superior people. Let's make them aristocrats, and their children after them, and their children after them. Blood will tell.

Director: Who will choose the superior people?

Lawyer: Superior people themselves.

Director: And who chooses them?

Lawyer: We'll establish a very small nucleus here and make it grow. Each new aristocrat will have a say.

Director: What does it take, a unanimous vote?

Lawyer: No, we'd never get anything done that way. Some kind of majority. We'd work it out.

Director: But isn't that a recipe for resentments right from the start? The ones who vote 'no' will resent the one who gets voted in despite them. And so on.

Lawyer: I told you aristocrats are jealous of one another. If you know of another way....

Director: What if you had a sort of leader in this—a philosopher, say?

Lawyer: What, the philosopher would make recommendations, then we'd vote?

Director: Yes. That might lessen the animosity among aristocrats, no? They'd blame the philosopher for selecting the would-be aristocrats in question, not their peers.

Lawyer: But their peers would still vote. Still, it might take out some of the sting. You have a point. But this philosopher would have to be an aristocrat himself.

Director: It takes one to know one? I'm pretty sure many democrats would be able to recognize aristocrats on sight.

Lawyer: It's because of the beauty. Everyone can sense human excellence.

Director: Then why not let the democrats choose?

Lawyer: What! Are you serious? Don't you know democrats resent aristocrats? They would choose their own to rule over them.

Director: What would these own be like?

Lawyer: At best? Quick and clever in thought, but not profound. In body sturdy, not elegant. In heart and soul, simple and lacking subtlety.

Director: Is that so bad?

Lawyer: No, if you're willing to sacrifice profundity, elegance, and subtlety. But these things are worth fighting for, Director. They're the beauty in life.

Director: So the people, the plebs, the many—are ugly?

Lawyer: Don't act surprised. And, yes, there can be beauty among them—but not a ruling beauty.

Director: So the beauty of profundity, subtlety, and elegance only comes into its own when it rules?

Lawyer: Yes. Rule puts those things into high relief.

Director: And none of those traits conflicts with the virtues needed for war.

Lawyer: Not only do they not conflict, they enhance the virtues of war. Wouldn't you fear a profoundly subtle enemy? How about elegant plans of battle? Do you see what I mean?

Director: Yes, I think I do. Aristocrats are simply the best. And the best should rule.

Lawyer: Yes.

Director: But democrats believe the best should rule. They elect them every year.

Lawyer: Like I said, they elect their own. True, that may be best for them. But we have to be willing to break with that.

Director: With the greatest good for the greatest number. That's a hard one to break. Do we really want to break it? Do we need to break it?

Lawyer: Look at it this way. Weeds outnumber flowers. Should we do the greatest good for the weeds? That makes no sense. We care for the flowers. We uproot the weeds.

Director: The many are weeds. Interesting.

Lawyer: It's not as bad as it sounds. Ask anyone if most people are good or bad, and you'll hear that most are rotten. The many know this about themselves.

Director: But aristocrats are rotten, too. Aren't they?

Lawyer: That's the prejudice of the many. They think that because most of the many are rotten, all others must mostly be rotten, too.

Director: And when the aristocrats are allowed to rule, they'll prove their worth.

Lawyer: Exactly.

Director: Their worth to the other aristocrats.

Lawyer: Yes, but the many will also benefit from being well led.

Director: The aristocrats will do them good?

Lawyer: Is that so strange? Here we have the natural order of things. Everyone benefits when put in their proper place.

Director: So you don't break with the idea of the greatest good for the greatest number. Aristocracy is that greatest good, with everyone in their place.

Lawyer: The hard part is getting the many to own up to this truth. Pride gets in their way.

Director: How do we do it now? I mean, the many don't rule in our democracy, do they? It's the super rich who do.

Lawyer: Well, the many see the rich as just like them, but rich. The rich play it up this way. It's what we said about justifying themselves to the many.

Director: Yes, the charade. How do we work with the pride of the many? Who likes being told they're second class?

Lawyer: Second class? They'd be third class. Second class are those from the many who prove their worth and work for the few.

Director: Who likes being told they're third class?

Lawyer: If you're born into that class, it doesn't sting as much.

Director: So what is it? One great big sting to put everyone where they belong, and then it's easier after that?

Lawyer: I can't see a better way. Not unless we drag this out as a gradual process over centuries.

Director: Maybe that way is best. But I must admit I have my doubts about the whole thing.

Lawyer: Oh? Why?

Director: I wonder about the fate of philosophy in all this. The fierce censorship in particular makes me doubt. Truth might be a casualty here.

Lawyer: And it isn't now? Isn't it the truth that some are better than others?

Director: I worry who will judge.

Lawyer: There will be mistakes, yes. But more often than not we'll get it right. A vast improvement over today.

Director: The people will always believe in democracy. What can you do? Actively suppress?

Lawyer: Suppress belief? I don't care what people believe—so long as they behave.

Director: Then why censor books and such?

Lawyer: Books rally people around them. That's not my idea of good behavior.

Director: Rallying is bad? Aristocrats don't rally?

Lawyer: You only rally when you've been set back. A good aristocracy is never set back.

Director: Then you haven't read your Thucydides. Aristocracies are constantly rallying. The many versus the few, the age-old conflict. Too bad for you we live in the age of the many.

15

Lawyer: Philosophers are few. Don't you hate this reign of the many?

Director: Well, maybe I spoke too fast. The extremely rich rule, not the many. Isn't that how it is?

Lawyer: It's an oligarchy. Aristocrats are the enemies of oligarchs.

Director: Enemies of the many; enemies of the extremely rich few. You're fighting on all sides.

Lawyer: Many of the extremely rich are crass.

Director: Why not ally with the many and fight the very rich few?

Lawyer: It's a question of expediency. The oligarchs make for powerful allies. They have a sympathy for the aristocratic few.

Director: A sympathy for those who look down on them?

Lawyer: When push comes to shove, few is few.

Director: But you care about things like virtue and beauty. Oligarchs don't.

Lawyer: They buy beauty whenever they can.

Director: They buy virtue whenever they can.

Lawyer: True. My virtue is not for sale.

Director: Then they'll never ally with you.

Lawyer: So we must fight our fight alone?

Director: That's how all fights are fought.

Lawyer: Philosophers fight alone?

Director: Maybe more so than you might imagine.

Lawyer: Aristocrats today can imagine fighting alone. Maybe that's why philosophers should best ally with them.

Director: I'm torn. Who doesn't want or need an ally? But most allies are at best fellow travelers.

Lawyer: Travel with me to suppress the many. You'll find it worthwhile.

Director: A philosopher I enjoy once said that commercial republics support philosophy best. Commerce and aristocracy are opposed.

Lawyer: There can be commerce in an aristocracy. The commercial just need to know their place.

Director: As philosophers should know their place?

Lawyer: Wouldn't you rather be an aristocrat than a philosopher?

Director: Are you offering me the job?

Lawyer: Would that it were mine to offer. But let's get back to commerce. The Venetian Republic lasted more than a thousand years. It was an oligarchy of aristocrats and very wealthy merchants. I'd be willing to compromise with something like that.

Director: So you are flexible. Well, we already have the very wealthy merchants. Now all we need are the aristocrats. But I thought the Venetians had a mixed regime, more mixed than what you describe. I thought I read that it had a democratic element in the state.

Lawyer: If I had to choose, I'd take the Venetian mix. Our democratic element is far too strong.

Director: So are you admitting a little mix is good? You're not looking for pure aristocracy?

Lawyer: Maybe a little mix is good. Pure aristocracies can get a little... severe.

Director: What might be the role of the people?

Lawyer: I would have them elect a committee from among themselves to oversee professional sports. People love sports.

Director: Aristocrats love sports. Won't they be jealous of the people's power here?

Lawyer: Aristocrats care about amateur sports, the sports they themselves play. The people won't be invited to play or watch.

Director: That creates a sort of mystique.

Lawyer: Exactly what we want. Aristocrats must take every chance to distance themselves from the plebs.

16

Director: So I take it there will be separate schools.

Lawyer: Of course there will be separate schools. There will be no mingling of the classes.

Director: Don't we have something like that now? Economically speaking.

Lawyer: We do. But it's not enough. And remember—aristocracy isn't based on money; it's based on excellence.

Director: But money follows naturally from excellence.

Lawyer: Yes, but you do see the importance of this point.

Director: Money is a support, a tool—not an end.

Lawyer: Precisely. Money helps with distance.

Director: Money helps with control.

Lawyer: True.

Director: So what happens if somewhere down the line a rich aristocratic family loses its excellence, its virtue? All it is is rich. Do you kick it out of the circle?

Lawyer: We can't let a mere oligarchy form. Oligarchy is the death of aristocracy, its opposite.

Director: Oligarchy means rule of the few. For you, they have to be the excellent few.

Lawyer: That's why I distinguish between mere oligarchy and aristocracy. The latter is rule of the best.

Director: Would you say what we have now is a plutocracy, a rule of the very rich?

Lawyer: Yes and no. No doubt the plutocrats are in power. But there really is a strong challenge from the democrats. They make it hard on the rich.

Director: Poor plutocrats. But you're something in the middle. You're not exceedingly rich, though you have plenty of money.

Lawyer: I'm not a billionaire, if that's what you mean. I have many millions, though. That creates great distance from the vast majority.

Director: How do you interact with the billionaires? You work for them, don't you?

Lawyer: I don't. I seek clients, and clients seek me, from my own level. I think there's such a thing as being too rich.

Director: Interesting. So how do you tame the billionaires?

Lawyer: If we can form an aristocracy of people like me, we turn on them.

Director: What does that mean?

Lawyer: We confiscate their assets and give them to the people.

Director: Now you really are surprising me. Why would you do that? To curry favor with the people?

Lawyer: Curry? No. We want to win their trust. And in turn, we want them to support our cause.

Director: The cause that shuts them out of rule. I don't know, Lawyer. Sign here for your check and sacrifice your power. Who would go for that?

Lawyer: People today don't believe they have much power. It will seem like a gift with no real strings attached.

Director: So your entire plan depends on corruption of our regime. It depends on the loss of power in the people.

Lawyer: Did you think that if the people were strong, an aristocracy could ever take shape? A weak people means bad government in a democracy. No one wants to live under bad government. When the people know things are bad, an aristocracy looks okay.

Director: Why not just retake their power?

Lawyer: Power once lost like this is lost for good. It's because of effects on the character.

Director: Can you say more?

Lawyer: Power is like muscles. Once you stop using them, they decay. Is it possible to gain them back? Yes. But it takes more effort than most are willing to make. And so they look to others to right the ship.

Director: Those others being you and your friends. But what do you do? Promise to take things back to what they were? Are aristocrats, at first at least, conservatives?

Lawyer: This is a difficult question. What does it mean to conserve? To preserve. Democrats are conservative concerning democracy, though they are often known to be progressive or liberal on social or fiscal policy.

Director: Your aristocrats would be revolutionary and then, once established, deeply and ruthlessly conservative. That's a difficult adjustment to make. Where does the revolution end and the conservation begin?

Lawyer: That's why we must have clearly defined goals from the outset. Once those goals are reach, no matter what, we must stop and conserve.

Director: I imagine there will be temptations to push things further, and further— just one more gain here, and another there.

Lawyer: Yes, you know exactly how it will go. We have to be firm. We must all take an oath that we will stop at a certain point. Otherwise there is no end.

Director: Does this mean you have to choose your aristocrats before the push begins? I mean, who would fight without knowing they're in?

Lawyer: That makes a good deal of sense. We would coordinate this all in advance.

Director: Will there be ranks within the aristocracy, or are all aristocrats equal?

Lawyer: All will be equal, but with distinctions for merit and roles to fill.

Director: Ambassador to Russia, for instance.

Lawyer: Right. Things like that.

Director: How will the ambassador be chosen? Is it by vote of equals?

Lawyer: Why not?

Director: Is that a democratic element in the aristocracy?

Lawyer: I suppose it is. The key is defining who is equal.

Director: What kind of ratio do you have in mind, aristocrats to population? One in ten? One in a hundred? One in a thousand? One in ten thousand?

Lawyer: I guess I never thought this through. Even one in ten lends distinction. But one in ten thousand makes you rare. Take a city of 300,000. There would be 30 aristocratic families. Is that enough to run the place?

Director: What about the lieutenant class you mentioned? Maybe there are 300 of them, ten for every aristocratic family.

Lawyer: Yes, we'll have to work this out.

Director: But there's a problem. Families grow. Your numbers will swell.

Lawyer: The head of the household rules. The rest are aristocrats, yes—but non-ruling members. It's not a problem.

Director: Maybe these non-ruling members could perform certain tasks to help run the show.

Lawyer: Yes, of course.

Director: Yes, that would be best. Too many unemployed aristocrats can be a source of trouble.

Lawyer: What kind of trouble? They'll cultivate themselves, as we said.

Director: Cultivation takes an effort, no? A great effort, even.

Lawyer: No doubt it does. Are you saying not everyone will be up to the task?

Director: Let's just say some people will need encouragement.

Lawyer: What, like school? I was thinking we might have no schools.

Director: Why?

Lawyer: We should encourage individualized learning, the best kind there is.

Director: Who will teach? Fellow aristocrats or an elite from the many?

Lawyer: Both, naturally. From one you can learn one sort of thing; from the other another.

Director: What can you learn from the pleb?

Lawyer: Specialized things.

Director: What do you mean?

Lawyer: No aristocrat is going to narrow his view to become a specialist in a certain subject matter.

Director: Not even if that matter piques his interest?

Lawyer: Aristocrats need knowledge of rule, the most general knowledge there is. It's fine to have a hobby in a certain area. But it never rises to the level of expertise.

Director: Are your aristocrats anti-intellectual?

Lawyer: Intellectuals as a class will no longer exist. Our teaching plebs will not be intellectuals, but rather masters of a certain craft.

Director: What's wrong with intellectuals?

Lawyer: They're always trying to win over the many.

Director: What if they were dedicated to the few?

Lawyer: Intellectuals think of themselves as above it all. Or rather, they think of themselves as equal to the best. We can't have that in our regime.

Director: So you have to ensure they gain no prestige, like any other group in your realm. Only aristocrats can have real prestige.

Lawyer: Do you think that's so bad? Pride and prestige are different things. All can have pride, potentially. Few can have prestige.

Director: What pride can the many have?

Lawyer: Men and women can always have pride, depending on how they carry themselves. But I was thinking about pride in our country.

Director: But it's your country, not theirs.

Lawyer: We need to manage things so that everyone belongs. Service in the armed forces can help the plebs with this.

Director: Why would they fight?

Lawyer: Why do men and women always fight? They fight for their families; they fight for their friends; they fight for the one next to them in the trench.

Director: Is that cynical?

Lawyer: It's practical. People will love our country because it contains their families, their friends, and the person next door. It's what they know. It is their own. People always love and fight for their own.

Director: So you can never interfere with that own-ness.

Lawyer: I wouldn't dream of it! That's where many aristocracies went wrong. They tyrannized over the many's family and friends. They didn't let the many be. I would let them be, and I would encourage them to grow.

Director: Within their proper sphere, of course.

Lawyer: Of course. The many need not be lowly. The many can be strong and proud within their place.

Director: What about intermarriages?

Lawyer: No problem. But the aristocrat sacrifices all rights, and none accrue to the pleb.

Director: Remind me, Lawyer. What's this all about?

Lawyer: Freedom. Freedom for the aristocrats. We claim we have freedom today, but that's a lie. The people are economic slaves. I am wealthy but work like a dog. Only the very few, the billionaires, have any semblance of freedom. But even they often have plebeian consciences that spur them ever on.

Director: Better to have the few free than none. Is that it?

Lawyer: That's exactly it. It's the best we can do. It really is for the sake of all humanity that freedom should truly exist.

Director: Are you going to tell me that the freedom of the few benefits the many?

Lawyer: Like I said before, we give them some hope that this freedom one day might be theirs, or their children's, or their children's children's. But it's not only about freedom. It's about rule. Rule is work—a chore, if you will. We relieve the people of that.

Director: That's generous of you. But if rule is really such a chore, what guarantee is there that the few will be up to the task?

Lawyer: Their love of excellence. Excellence in rule brings the highest honor. Aristocrats are driven by honor above all else. That's our guarantee.

Director: What makes one person honor driven and another not?

Lawyer: I don't know. But I know the difference when I see it.

Director: You prefer to be around honor-driven souls?

Lawyer: I do. It makes me up my game.

Director: You simply want to be the best. But when your whole class wants to be the best, that must spell trouble. No?

Lawyer: I'm not going to lie. Aristocrats are sometimes at odds over who is best.

Director: Sometimes? I would think it happens all the time. What do you do with someone who behaves very badly after a loss?

Lawyer: If it's very bad, we cast them out for a time. This lets them cool down.

Director: Or stew in their juices for a while.

19

Lawyer: It's a problem. What can I say? But if the problem is that people are trying their best and get frustrated when they're not the best, there are worse problems to have.

Director: Meaning the many don't try.

Lawyer: Many of the many don't try. But a few, a significant few, of the many try.

Director: The lieutenant class and such.

Lawyer: Exactly. We reward their effort. And since the few are few, there is a need for many lieutenants.

Director: Opportunity abounds.

Lawyer: Opportunity for many today is a lie. We'll be more honest.

Director: No American Dream?

Lawyer: We'll deal in realities, not dreams. Besides, who are the dreamers in this land? They always try to get ahead. They snatch up every slight chance, every little advantage. They know nothing but work and the next step ahead. It's pathetic, if you ask me.

Director: You'd take that away?

Lawyer: Ha! And it would be a blessing!

Director: What would you replace it with, in your lieutenancy?

Lawyer: Measured work, not endless toil. Opportunity to interact with the best. Security of place.

Director: Security of place? But couldn't they be dismissed over a whim?

Lawyer: We'll take a long time to vet these people. Once chosen odds are good we've made a good choice. And we'll grow attached to them. We wouldn't dismiss them over a whim.

Director: But there's no guarantee.

Lawyer: No, no guarantee.

Director: Why not?

Lawyer: Because aristocrats must rule. And to rule means to have the freedom to rule. If you can't rule your own staff, what can you rule?

Director: Are there laws in your aristocracy?

Lawyer: What, you mean do we have the rule of law? I suppose there will be a charter establishing the aristocratic families. But beyond that? No. If law rules, the rulers don't rule. And we ourselves ruling will make us so much more flexible than if bound by law.

Director: The flexible aristocrat. That's quite a thing. Flexible here, yes; but not when it comes to censorship.

Lawyer: Oh, we're only going to filter out the trash. Your philosophical works will stand.

Director: Even the ones that question aristocracy?

Lawyer: Why question aristocracy?

Director: Philosophers often question the current regime.

Lawyer: But not if they see the beauty of that regime. Better for them to question what the aristocrats think.

Director: Aristocrats think aristocracy is best.

Lawyer: I'm thinking about things of beauty. Aesthetics is a lost science. Maybe you could bring it back. There's honor in that, you know.

Director: Thank you for providing me with a field of honor. I'll have to give it some thought. But philosophy questions the unquestionable. Tell philosophy it can't question here, and it will find a way to question precisely there.

Lawyer: Are you saying you could never live in an aristocracy?

Director: No, I'm not saying that. But there would be friction.

Lawyer: I'd expect nothing less! Friction can be good. It promotes thought. And aristocrats should think about themselves from time to time.

Director: As a sort of self-help?

Lawyer: Why not?

20

Director: What if the friction is bad, annoying, tiresome? What then?

Lawyer: You have to be tactful, Director. It's the same in a democracy. You can't just go around rubbing everyone the wrong way.

Director: Do you think certain people deserve to be rubbed wrong?

Lawyer: There are people I'd like to see rubbed wrong—the crusading, resentful egalitarians, for instance. Why don't you practice on them?

Director: While there may be exceptions, the type doesn't appeal.

Lawyer: You only talk with those who appeal?

Director: Well, sometimes I'm forced at work. But when I have a choice? Of course I only talk with those who appeal to me, friend.

Lawyer: If I'm an aristocrat, and you're not—tell me what appeals.

Director: I, too, have a concern with human excellence. Philosophy is concerned.

Lawyer: The philosophy of excellence. I like it. What makes someone excellent?

Director: He or she does very well. What do you think? A good definition?

Lawyer: To excel means to surpass, exceed. To go beyond the others. Those who go beyond end up together. A natural class.

Director: So someone who excels in football is an aristocrat at heart.

Lawyer: Well, no. Not that.

Director: How about someone who excels at law?

Lawyer: That's more the thing.

Director: Why law and not football?

Lawyer: The excellence has to do with politics.

Director: You don't think there are politics in football?

Lawyer: Oh, I'm sure there are. But it's not the same sort of thing. The excellence has to do with the state—your ability to contribute toward the state.

Director: You're talking about the art of rule.

Lawyer: I am. And if a football player knows the art of rule, he may well be an aristocrat at heart.

Director: What does it mean to rule?

Lawyer: To exercise power or authority over others.

Director: And only certain people are qualified in this.

Lawyer: Absolutely. That's the benefit of aristocracy. You are guaranteed good rule.

Director: Guaranteed?

Lawyer: Sure. Not perfect rule. Good rule. It's in the aristocrats' interest. It's in everyone's interest. Better to be a pleb in a well run aristocracy than a democrat in a poorly run state.

Director: That's interesting. I never looked at it that way before.

Lawyer: What do you mean?

Director: Poorly run. Poorly. Poorly run means run by the poor. I wonder if that's the etymology. It's the opposite of richly run. I'd like to be a member of a richly run state. Oh wait, I am.

Lawyer: Believe me, I'm no fan of most of the rich. They spend their efforts not in pursuit of excellence but in grubbing for money. Whatever makes the most money, that's what they'll do. Whatever makes the most money, that's what they value. Whoever makes the most money, that's who is wise. I want aristocrats to have money, not earn it.

Director: How refreshingly honest. To have but not to earn. So wealth should be inherited.

Lawyer: Certainly. I don't want a money grubbing thought to ever enter my descendants' minds. Only noble thoughts. Only noble deeds. I want them to have a certain elevation. I know you can understand. I've never sensed a single grubbing thought in you.

21

Director: It's as you said. Money is a tool.

Lawyer: It's beneath our dignity to value making money.

Director: What is money?

Lawyer: It's a kind of belief, belief in value. It says when I give you dollars, or whatever the currency is, I value what you'll offer me in return.

Director: Fix your plumbing, for instance.

Lawyer: Sure, or put a new roof on my house. And when someone pays me to do something, I believe in the value of what I'm given.

Director: You believe your work, or whatever, is appreciated.

Lawyer: Yes. Appreciation. That's the thing. But that's also the problem. People believe in money so much that they allow it to become their self-esteem. People give me money; they believe in me; so I must be worth something after all! But that's such an empty way to look at the world. Don't you agree?

Director: I do. But can you really buy self-esteem with all the money you earn?

Lawyer: Yes, you certainly can. Ask ruling class America. But the more common illness among the American few is that they debase themselves. They justify themselves in the terms of the common man. They love to claim that anyone can do what they've done—but they're not exactly clear on just what they've done.

Director: What have they done?

Lawyer: Sold out their noble selves.

Director: Are you about to tell me that the common man can have a noble self?

Lawyer: Do you really think you'd catch me in that? Of course not. Nobility is bred, not earned. When you're noble, you can't help being noble.

Director: So for the others it's just too bad.

Lawyer: We haven't spoken of happiness. I believe that in a noble regime the plebs can be happy even if the nobility is not.

Director: That's quite a thing to think. Would you rather be noble than happy?

Lawyer: I certainly would. Happiness is a lesser state than satisfaction. Nobles are satisfied.

Director: How?

Lawyer: Through excellent rule.

Director: Are you talking about servant leaders? Do you know what I mean?

Lawyer: I no doubt do. This is one of the thorniest problems I've encountered. What does excellent rule mean? What's the purpose of rule? Xenophon wrote about this in his Life of Cyrus.

Director: In the Greek it's The Education of Cyrus. Was Cyrus happy?

Lawyer: I don't think he was. But he was a very excellent ruler.

Director: What made him excellent?

Lawyer: He was a great leader in war. He always thought of his people. He founded a terribly great empire. He was satisfied in this.

Director: Is that how you'd be in your rule over the Americans of the future?

Lawyer: The Americans are spoiled. Nuclear weapons bought them an empire at a fraction of its cost.

Director: Technology takes great effort.

Lawyer: Science, bah. Or should I say technology, bah? Science feeds technology, and there's no respect in either one.

Director: Respect for the noble.

Lawyer: Right. What's the purpose of discovery after discovery? Are we happier now than we were then, before science, before Bacon and his shameless promotion of the Advancement of Learning?

Director: Advancement of learning isn't noble?

Lawyer: No! It's all about science this and science that. Science is plebeian in spirit! Science knows no noble flights. Science plods along accumulating fact after fact until it concludes something banal.

Director: But those conclusions all add up.

22

Lawyer: Let's ask this. Are scientists happy?

Director: I think it depends on the scientist, for reasons other than science itself.

Lawyer: Yes, I think that's true. But are scientists satisfied? As scientists.

Director: I don't think they are.

Lawyer: Why not?

Director: Because if it's fact after fact there's always—always—another fact. Unless they stop and rest on their laurels.

Lawyer: What laurels? Someone cured cancer? Great, but it's not that simple. There are different kinds of cancer, and no one cures it all at once.

Director: But if they did? Satisfaction?

Lawyer: No, there's always another step to take.

Director: How does it differ with the few?

Lawyer: Are you suggesting the scientists are few?

Director: The great ones are.

Lawyer: Don't get me started. There is nothing—nothing—noble about science. Science would tear the noble down.

Director: Why?

Lawyer: Because nobility is of the spirit, and science has no truck there.

Director: What about psychology?

Lawyer: Name me a single proven thing psychology has learned.

Director: How about psychiatry?

Lawyer: That's a more interesting thing. Psychiatry has some proven chemical insights into the spirit. It deserves some respect. But we're only talking about being useful to the sick.

Director: Can there be a noble psychiatry?

Lawyer: Can there be noble general practitioners? It's the same question. The answer is no. They are technicians of the body, no more.

Director: But what if they ruled their patients? Aristocrats of sorts?

Lawyer: You don't have to obey a doctor, no matter what they like to think with their doctor's orders and all. So doctors really don't rule. Sure, you might say that those committed to mental institutions are ruled. But who really wants to rule under such conditions? Not I.

Director: Nor I. But who rules the soul?

Lawyer: It used to be priests. Who rules now? I find it hard to say.

Director: Is it just anyone who holds sway over the spirit?

Lawyer: Yes, I guess it's a sort of petty rule. For some people it's fathers or mothers; for others it's friends; for others still it's artists of sorts. You can imagine the rest.

Director: Can some of these rulers be noble?

Lawyer: Absolutely, yes. But it doesn't happen that often.

Director: Do they deserve to be promoted into the nobility?

Lawyer: No, but that's an interesting question. Does anyone tend to spiritual needs in an aristocracy? Is there some sort of Church? That's what used to happen to second sons, you know. They either went into the Church or the Law.

Director: Maybe Psychology is the Church.

Lawyer: I don't know. That frightens me a little. I've never trusted psychologists. They always seemed to me to need their own services more than I did.

Director: It used to be a commonplace that priests were the ones who needed most to be saved. Let's forget about a Church for your regime. And we've already forgotten about the Law. There is nothing but the rule of heads of family. But I have to ask. Are the heads men only or are you thinking of women, too?

Lawyer: Women can be excellent rulers. They can be heads.

Director: But how do you choose in a family where both show excellent traits?

23

Lawyer: Maybe we have a vote by all the heads of the state. Maybe this happens with each family no matter what. That way things are firm and fair.

Director: It certainly cuts down on the chances of things going wrong because of someone unfit taking the reins. What else do you have to consider that might go wrong?

Lawyer: Wastrels.

Director: Even if everyone is chosen by the heads?

Lawyer: Sometimes you're forced to choose the lesser of two evils.

Director: What's wrong with wastrels? What happens?

Lawyer: They run through their money. A poor aristocrat is a dangerous aristocrat.

Director: A danger to himself, his peers, the state, and the plebs?

Lawyer: Yes.

Director: Is there anything to be done?

Lawyer: Not without curbing the freedoms of all the peers. All we can hope is that we'll nip the behavior in the bud.

Director: I suppose the danger is greatest in the second generation.

Lawyer: That's an excellent observation. The first generation will be hand chosen. But the generation after that? Many will not have experienced upbringing in a fully aristocratic regime. Suppose the head is chosen at age fifty when the aristocracy starts. He might have a son aged twenty-five. Too late to raise him in the regime. Yes, the second generation is the key. With some luck we're golden.

Director: Maybe you need to vet entire families and not just heads.

Lawyer: Yes, you might be right. I'll have to give this some thought.

Director: The total regime.

Lawyer: Oh, stop. Excellence takes total commitment. You know that.

Director: So what happens when you can't totally commit?

Lawyer: What do you mean?

Director: I mean, here you are living in a democracy—the greatest democracy ever, some would say. Surely you're not free to pursue a life of excellence. So what do you do?

Lawyer: I do the next best thing. I pave the way for future excellence. That's why I wanted to talk to you today. I think you can help.

Director: How? Who wouldn't like to open the way to excellence? What can I do?

Lawyer: We want you to write.

Director: We? Who is we? Is this the royal you?

Lawyer: Don't worry about who we are for now. Let's just say your talents have been noted and admired.

Director: Are you inviting me to join a conspiracy?

Lawyer: No. We're looking for inspiration. As you said, we live in a democracy. This can, to put it mildly, get natural aristocrats down. We'd like you to start with something small—an essay on the virtues of aristocracy.

Director: You would do a better job at that than I. After all, you are a wonderful writer. Your legal briefs persuade and you win cases. I can't claim to do that. You are, in a very real sense, a professional writer. I am amateur at best.

Lawyer: Director, we need all the help we can get.

Director: Well, let me think. We've already discussed many of aristocracy's virtues. Maybe there's one...

Lawyer: One what?

Director: ...that surpasses all the rest.

Lawyer: It has to be excellence.

Director: Yes, but excellence in service of something. I know! Excellence in service of philosophy!

Lawyer: How?

Director: You carve out a small space for philosophy, a place in the heart of the regime. Your inner most, inner most circle.

Lawyer: And then do what?

Director: Nothing. Just let philosophy be. Don't interfere. Don't ask for propaganda. Just let it be.

24

Lawyer: And that's the purpose, the end of aristocracy?

Director: I can't think of one better.

Lawyer: What will come of this?

Director: Maybe nothing. Maybe something. I don't know. I depends on what you take away from the philosopher.

Lawyer: Hold on. One philosopher?

Director: Yes. And I won't be shy in saying it should be me. Or maybe you know of a better philosopher?

Lawyer: I don't. But wouldn't you want company?

Director: That's why I want to be in the heart of the regime. I want devotees of excellence as my friends. I won't cost much to maintain—just food, clothing, and shelter. Well, maybe some good wine now and then.

Lawyer: But don't you want the company of other philosophers?

Director: One philosopher per regime is enough. Besides, I will have the youth to train.

Lawyer: Train them in excellence.

Director: No. That's up to you. I will train them in philosophy, a philosophy that helps steer the regime.

Lawyer: Yes, but you can't simply be given free rein. Steering the state is a political matter.

Director: That's why I'll teach political philosophy. Oh, I'll confer with you and your friends and together we'll set the tone. But there is one important caveat. I won't help you establish the regime.

Lawyer: You'll just step in after the fact?

Director: Yes.

Lawyer: You're looking for a very sweet deal.

Director: I am. If you don't succeed, I go about my business. If you do, I'm yours.

Lawyer: That's not a very noble way of looking at things, if you don't mind my saying.

Director: If aristocracy is a *fait accompli*, I will accept what necessity sends my way. That's the best I can offer.

Lawyer: So you don't think aristocracy is inherently best.

Director: The best political regime? With a little mix of other elements of government, I think it is. But what does it mean to be the best in this? It's best for the state, not necessarily the people living in it.

Lawyer: I thought we agreed the many must sacrifice for the few.

Director: I'm talking about the aristocrats.

Lawyer: How can it not be best for them?

Director: Philosophy is what's best for us. Philosophy has no rockier road than in an aristocracy that has been properly mixed.

Lawyer: I don't understand. Why? Isn't philosophy inherently concerned with excellence?

Director: Philosophy is concerned with belief. What will your aristocrats believe? Have you given that thought?

Lawyer: What's to believe? Excellence is... excellence!

Director: What if your peers believe they are excellent when they're not. Would they like philosophy to point out this flaw?

Lawyer: I would. You can be honest with me. And I can say with certainty you can be honest with us.

Director: That's good. It's a first step.

Lawyer: A first step toward what?

Director: Living a life devoted to philosophy.

Lawyer: Are philosophy and excellence the same?

Director: You tell me.

Lawyer: Philosophy defines what excellence, the noble is. But that doesn't mean it's noble itself.

Director: True. In fact, philosophy is a-noble.

Lawyer: But not anti-noble.

Director: No, not anti-noble. A-noble. Philosophy is neutral here.

Lawyer: But how can it be neutral if it's trying to steer the ship?

Director: Philosophy isn't saying, 'Here is the destination!' It leaves that to you. But it can say, 'Here there are reefs. Here there are rocks. Open water is that way ahead.'.

Lawyer: I like that. You trust aristocrats to know where to go.

Director: I trust many people to know where to go. It's the few who don't know that concern me.

25

Lawyer: You would train aristocrats to trust their instincts.

Director: Yes, but only after having questioned their instincts.

Lawyer: Why would you question an instinct?

Director: It might not be yours.

Lawyer: Ah. False instincts. Instincts imposed by others. Yes, I know what you mean. Can't you see that aristocracy fights these falsities?

Director: How?

Lawyer: By its alliance with philosophy!

Director: Perhaps—so long as it truly stays allied, and doesn't introduce falsities of its own.

Lawyer: I expect no less of you than to keep us honest.

Director: I'll do my best—so long as the dishonest don't do me in.

Lawyer: You have my word—I would not let that happen.

Director: But listen to us! We're speaking as if aristocracy is just around the corner.

Lawyer: Maybe it's closer than we think.

Director: How would it happen? I can't see it happening for centuries or longer.

Lawyer: It would have to happen in fact before it happens in name.

Director: How would it happen in fact?

Lawyer: We'd have to undermine the super rich.

Director: How?

Lawyer: We get the democrats to place a limit on wealth.

Director: So now the super rich are merely rich. Do you try to win them to the cause?

Lawyer: They'd never forgive us. No, we'd encourage them to leave.

Director: Encourage? Would you... threaten them?

Lawyer: In a quiet way, yes. We need them to leave. Maybe we even let them keep some of their money if they go.

Director: Okay. So now you are the rich. What happens next?

Lawyer: This is where I always get stuck. The people's habits are democratic. It takes a long time to change a habit. Do you have any suggestions?

Director: You have to get them to depend on you. How you do that, I don't know. But if you're talking about changing habits, you're going to need some kind of major catastrophe or fundamental change if you think it will happen in your lifetime.

Lawyer: Then maybe I do have to settle for being an opener of the way. I'll concentrate all my efforts on how to change democratic habits.

Director: Democracy means the people rule. How do you take rule away from someone?

Lawyer: You show them that it's a lie. They don't have rule. They have a worthless vote.

Director: And if they take the bait?

Lawyer: You ask them what they want with their vote. They'll say they want good government. We have to show them that comes with us.

Director: So here's the thing. Are you just going to deceive them? Let them think aristocracy is in their interest when it's not? Or do you believe aristocracy serves everyone best?

Lawyer: This is the crux. The lawyer in me can make the case that it's best for all. Is it? We have to make clear one thing. Aristocracies are founded on class—noble, ignoble. These are two fundamentally different kinds of human beings. This is what we have to believe.

Director: Do you believe it? Honestly, in your heart?

Lawyer: I... don't know. I've been conditioned to think we're all the same. Rationally, I know we're not.

26

Director: But what's in your heart?

Lawyer: My heart is torn. But not when I see these crazy radical egalitarians of the left. And not when I see low class parasites feeding off of the state.

Director: Your mention of the left makes me wonder. You don't consider yourself part of the right, do you?

Lawyer: While there are a number of closeted aristocrats on the right, no—I don't consider myself part of the right. I'm not a conservative. What would I conserve? A few hundred years of democracy? I don't fall on someone's political spectrum. I stand on my own.

Director: But if you had to classify yourself?

Lawyer: I'm a progressive. Progress is made every step closer we get to aristocracy. How's that?

Director: Funny. But are you sure you want to limit the benefits of progress to the nobility? Don't you want to sell the plebs on them, too?

Lawyer: What are our choices? Sell them into aristocracy? Trick them into aristocracy? Or force them into aristocracy? Can you think of anything else?

Director: Well, it may be quibbling but I would say you should distinguish between sell and persuade. Persuade them into aristocracy.

Lawyer: I think it would take a crisis for that.

Director: Things are so bad that they grant you control? Things would have to be pretty bad. But what about the other options? Trick them? How?

Lawyer: Oh, I don't know. Make false promises I suppose.

Director: And forcing them? This begs the question of the military.

Lawyer: Maybe in several centuries the military will be very unlike what it is today. Maybe it will be like it was in parts of Herbert's Dune—hand-to-hand combat.

Director: What does that have to do with aristocracy?

Lawyer: Natural fighters enhanced by early training will assume leadership. The seeds of aristocracy.

Director: I think you have a point. There will have to be a military component to what you're about. So do you want your regime to be dedicated to war? Is that the noble thing you'd strive toward with all your might?

Lawyer: You're probably laughing looking at me now, thinking I couldn't fight to save my life. Well, there was a time when I could.

Director: Is prowess in fighting the excellence you seek?

Lawyer: No. But it's what gets us in the door.

Director: What is higher than fighting?

Lawyer: Art, in every form. I include philosophy in this.

Director: As an art of words, an art of argument? I still want philosophy in the core of the regime.

Lawyer: You'd have to be able to fight. Not too many philosophers can claim excellence here.

Director: I can fight.

Lawyer: Do you know why it matters?

Director: Tell me.

Lawyer: A philosopher has to be able to hold his own in every sense. True?

Director: True. But there is hand-to-hand fighting with knives, and then there is the fight of character and words.

Lawyer: That's what you can teach—how to fight this way.

Director: Words can call character into doubt. Is there anything an aristocrat would hate more?

Lawyer: No, calling someone's character into question is the ultimate attack.

Director: Would I be challenged to a duel? Would you allow duels?

Lawyer: We need to say more about honor.

27

Director: What's to say? What is honor?

Lawyer: Your honor is your worth. There's your own sense of worth, then there's your worth in others' eyes.

Director: Which is the most dangerous to challenge?

Lawyer: That's a hard question. Challenge someone's worth in others' eyes and you're playing with fire. Challenge someone's own sense of worth and you just might cause a nuclear explosion.

Director: Well, I always go for the biggest bang for my buck. Besides, I think it's safer for a philosopher to challenge someone's own sense of worth. People get crazy when they think others might think less of them.

Lawyer: It's a very dangerous game to provoke some like this.

Director: That's why philosophers are few and far between. Not everyone is up to the challenge.

Lawyer: What's the outcome of the challenge?

Director: A stronger sense of self.

Lawyer: You know, I think that's very important for an aristocrat to have. In order to rule, to command, you need to have command of your self.

Director: No aristocrat can rule well without rule of self. I can help you here.

Lawyer: I don't doubt it. And we need the help now more than ever. What did you think of the riots this summer?

Director: People are scared.

Lawyer: The police are scared. They need to know they have our support.

Director: Are things getting to be bad enough that aristocracy might be possible? Is that what you're suggesting?

Lawyer: If we support the police, it's only natural to think they might support us. In this I include the national guard.

Director: And if the national guard?

Lawyer: Maybe the army, too.

Director: Your progressives might be closer to rule than we thought.

Lawyer: But how can we be sure?

Director: Talk to more philosophers.

Lawyer: What can they do?

Director: Make clear whether you're dreaming or on the cusp of something terrible.

Lawyer: Terrible?

Director: Regime change is terrible, even if it's not overtly violent. A new regime does violence to old ways of thought.

Lawyer: It's funny to think of democracy as an old way of thought. But I think you're right.

Director: You should avoid all unnecessary violence—physical, mental, whatever.

Lawyer: Is that how you justify what we'll do?

Director: What do you mean?

Lawyer: Do you say to yourself there is less violence overall in a move to aristocracy than there is in a trying to keep democracy afloat?

Director: You think it all comes down to violence?

Lawyer: Don't you?

Director: What is higher than violence?

Lawyer: Nobility.

Director: What is higher than nobility?

Lawyer: Philosophy. Do you agree?

Director: I'm not sure. There's something fascist that way.

Lawyer: You wouldn't be the first fascist philosopher.

Director: No, that's true.

28

Lawyer: But I don't think philosophy is higher than nobility. I don't think anything is.

Director: Then how do you steer the ship of state? What is your guiding light?

Lawyer: What was the Spartan guiding light?

Director: Obedience to their ancient laws. Is that what you want for yours?

Lawyer: We spoke of not having laws. Do you think that makes us inferior?

Director: No, I think you would surpass the Spartans in this.

Lawyer: That's almost too much to hope for.

Director: Don't be modest now. It doesn't become you. Dare to be different; dare to know.

Lawyer: That's interesting. By knowing we are different.

Director: Of course. Who knows?

Lawyer: The few. But the many know many things.

Director: About their own experience. But you have more mental leverage.

Lawyer: Mental leverage! Yes! I know exactly what you mean. Imagination coupled with daring thought.

Director: That's your guiding star.

Lawyer: The highest thing. Not imagination by itself. Not thought alone. The coupling. Dare I say it?

Director: Say it to me. What have you got to lose?

Lawyer: Thought impregnates imagination.

Director: And gives birth to what?

Lawyer: Hope.

Director: This is the province of the few?

Lawyer: Some of the many can think like this—artists, and so on. We will give them a special place.

Director: But not in the nobility.

Lawyer: No, not in the nobility.

Director: These people will stir your imagination and help you think?

Lawyer: They will. Just as we nobles will stir and help each other as a matter of course. It's just nice to have some outside inspiration now and then.

Director: Will these outsiders inspire the many?

Lawyer: We have to be careful here. We all need some hope. But the many cannot hope to rule. Ever.

Director: So it seems these outsiders will have to sing different tunes—one to the few, another to the many. And maybe one they sing to themselves.

Lawyer: As long as they keep it to themselves, that's fine—sing whatever they want. But yes, the song of the few differs from the song of the many.

Director: So there would have to be, for instance, two art galleries—one for the few, and one for the many.

Lawyer: Yes. Absolutely.

Director: And different books. And so on.

Lawyer: Right. That's how it has to be. And this doesn't hurt the many in any way. It just limits their scope.

Director: What about history? Two different histories here?

Lawyer: It's as it is with everything else. True history for us; romanticized history for them.

Director: You don't want romanticized history for your nobles?

Lawyer: We'll rule better if we have the truth.

29

Director: Why can't the people have the truth? Are the nobles taking advantage of them? Is that what you're trying to hide?

Lawyer: No, that's not it. We want the people to carry on as before. They will work, have families, enjoy their time off. Our noble books will describe them as lacking excellence. That can only be upsetting.

Director: And you really believe they'll be without excellence?

Lawyer: We've mentioned that there will be exceptions, but yes. Excellence is instilled and cultivated. In the case of excellence of rule, you need opportunity to practice. The plebs won't have the chance. The aristocrats will from earliest age on up. It's a total way of life.

Director: And you really think things can be for the people the way they are now?

Lawyer: I do. The only difference is that they won't choose their leaders.

Director: What about taxes?

Lawyer: They'll pay them as they pay them now.

Director: But the money will go to the few.

Lawyer: Of course. This is how we'll sustain ourselves. Each noble family will receive a certain amount of money each year. The rest will go to run the regime.

Director: But the people will know they're supporting you. Why go along? They resent taxes as it is.

Lawyer: Maybe there has to be a certain amount of... force.

Director: You punish those who don't pay. You create a culture of fear.

Lawyer: Have aristocrats ruled in any other way?

Director: I don't know. But what you say makes sense. But is it fear, like we fear the IRS; or is it terror?

Lawyer: There can be no room for doubt. Terror. Aristocracy requires a certain ruthlessness. After all, look how outnumbered aristocrats are.

Director: The people aren't as cruel.

Lawyer: Oh, I don't know about that. The people can be very cruel. Imagine what they'd do to us if they overthrew the regime!

Director: So it really is us versus them. There is no common interest.

Lawyer: We can lie and say there is, if that's what we think is best. I suppose it's in our interest for the plebs to stay relatively content so there's no unrest or lack of tax money coming in.

Director: A thriving economy is good for all parties involved. After all, it's life as usual for the people under the aristocracy, as you say—with a few important exceptions.

Lawyer: If we're wise, we'll keep the exceptions to a minimum.

Director: But you'll suspend elections.

Lawyer: No, we need to keep them in place. But they'll be electing their ambassadors, or what have you, to us. It's important for them to feel they have some control. We must change as little as possible here. Maybe we even let then have a president, who answers to us.

Director: You want to keep the communication between the classes to a minimum.

Lawyer: Yes. Let us be mysterious figures to them.

Director: Shadow lords.

Lawyer: Indeed. But among ourselves we are daylight clear.

Director: So everything seems normal except for your rule.

Lawyer: And isn't that how it is now? The super rich rule. We're swapping us for them. No more, no less.

Director: Why do people put up with the rule of the super rich?

Lawyer: For one, it's only in fact, not in name.

Director: Why does that matter?

Lawyer: It saves the plebs a certain amount of face.

Director: But your way would take that face away. The super rich can claim to be living the American Dream. Everyone has a chance, they say, at the American Dream.

Lawyer: And the people will have that chance under us. We shouldn't care how rich someone gets so long as they understand the nobility rules.

Director: Terror once again?

Lawyer: Yes.

30

Director: It's funny to think of someone ruling over the rich. Today no one does. Well, maybe the law.

Lawyer: The super rich make the laws, so it works out to their advantage—so long as they don't do anything stupid. I think I'd enjoy ruling the super rich. There's a delicious irony there.

Director: So you won't send them away?

Lawyer: No, I think we must. They'd never go along.

Director: So the aristocrats rule, but through go-betweens—those elected by the people.

Lawyer: Yes, the go-betweens are the lightning rods that keep strikes away from us.

Director: Yes, that's probably wise. So these go-betweens serve two masters—you and the plebs. A difficult position.

Lawyer: They have two masters now—the people and the super rich. We're substituting aristocrats for the super rich. That's a better way.

Director: Why? What makes it better?

Lawyer: Excellence. Humanity.

Director: Humanity? I thought you'd use terror.

Lawyer: On those who deserve it, sure. But we will have excellent judgment when it comes to character. We can help settle disputes very well.

Director: So you will be judges?

Lawyer: Why not? Can you think of better judges? I think we need to be judges. We can't trust judges from the people to make the right calls.

Director: Calls that support the aristocracy.

Lawyer: What else?

Director: But now I'm confused. We said there would be no laws.

Lawyer: No laws among the nobility. But for the people? There will be plenty of laws. Laws even of their own making.

Director: The illusion of self-rule.

Lawyer: Well, in a way, it would be self-rule. But instead of taking their bearings from the Constitution, the judges will take their bearings from us, with what supports human excellence among the ruling class.

Director: But what can laws among the people do for the ruling class?

Lawyer: There can be no laws that subvert our control. Do they want universal health care? Who cares? Let them have what they want.

Director: But you control the tax money.

Lawyer: Their leaders will know how much they'll have to spend. Remember, we're not trying to get filthy rich off of this arrangement. We simply want enough to live on in comfort without money as a worry.

Director: Definitions of comfort vary.

Lawyer: True. Think of Sparta again; a Spartan lifestyle would suit us best.

Director: The Spartans were notorious hoarders of gold.

Lawyer: Well, as we said—we'll be better than them. So if the people want to spend their money on healthcare, fine. If they want to legalize marijuana? Fine. If they want free and legal abortion? Fine. Whatever they want so long as it doesn't interfere with us.

Director: You'll let them use up their energies this way.

Lawyer: Exactly so. So let us live in our separate spheres and keep away from each other as much as we can. And things might work out very well indeed.

31

Director: So as far as aristocrats go, you won't be ruling very much. You'll get money from the people, and you'll have final say over what they do. But you'll let them live their own lives.

Lawyer: Yes, and that's what makes this work. Besides, if an exceptional pleb comes along, we reward them with a position.

Director: Lieutenants, as you said.

Lawyer: Sure, and other positions, too.

Director: How does this work? Do you tell the president to make the appointment, and not reveal your hand? Or do you make the appointment yourself?

Lawyer: Best to let the president do it and keep our hand in this obscured. That way they feel more independence than they have.

Director: The more real or seeming independence you can give them, the better this all works.

Lawyer: Precisely. Let's keep the plebs happy and rule the land.

Director: The land. Aristocracies in the past were based on land. Yours is based on taxes from a sham democracy.

Lawyer: Different times require different means. But is it really a sham? How is the life of an individual citizen changed?

Director: Knowledge that there is a group above changes everything.

Lawyer: That's why we must severely limit our interactions with them. Let them forget. And trust me—people forget. They forget the super rich today. They hardly have a democracy now. Just look at the Electoral College! What's the purpose of that?

Director: Aren't we becoming more democratic every day? Doesn't improved and enhanced communication make this inevitable?

Lawyer: It puts pressure on those in power to be more responsive and transparent. But no one can bear to be fully responsive and transparent. No one. It's an impossibility. So democrats are demanding the impossible. They are backing those in power into a corner. That's dangerous.

Director: But it creates opportunity for you.

Lawyer: We can ally with the people and drive those in power out. Our terms, to begin with, are simply the tax to support ourselves.

Director: People will never go for that.

Lawyer: Oh, we won't call ourselves aristocrats. We'll be political mercenaries of a sort. Look how much money government spends on consulting, whatever that means. Well, we'll be consultants of sorts. We'll facilitate the elimination of those in power.

Director: Elimination?

Lawyer: However the people want them disposed, we'll dispose.

Director: And then?

Lawyer: We set ourselves up as a sort of oversight committee. The people elect new leaders and we settle in. Then we begin to train our young.

Director: How long do you think you'll exist as a committee?

Lawyer: Maybe we always exist with that name. Why provoke by calling ourselves something the people didn't establish? Who cares if we go down in history as The Committee?

Director: It reminds me of another famous committee, The Committee of Public Safety in the French Revolution. It employed terror.

Lawyer: But for a bad end.

Director: Do you need the people to encourage you to commit acts of terror?

Lawyer: We can uncover plots against the people and eliminate the conspirators.

Director: And there will be a crescendo of plots and terror against the conspirators?

Lawyer: Naturally. Emergency powers will eventually be required.

Director: And when you have them?

Lawyer: We are given provisional control of the military to help us in our work.

Director: And to maintain order.

Lawyer: Of course.

Director: Why would people trust you?

Lawyer: They sense our love of excellence. Part of that excellence is honesty, integrity, and trustworthiness. This isn't a sham. The traits are real. People feel this. And in desperate times they turn to us.

32

Director: But your provisional control becomes permanent control. Excellent.

Lawyer: The more I think about this, the more I realize we have to come to power honestly.

Director: So you need conditions in the democracy to be bad.

Lawyer: Yes. We must make a natural transition to aristocracy. Any other way and we undermine ourselves. Can I teach honesty and integrity to my children when they know I stole the state?

Director: You can, but you'd be a hypocrite.

Lawyer: I don't want to be a hypocrite.

Director: You don't want a founding lie.

Lawyer: No, I don't.

Director: So your Committee of Oversight is established. I suppose at that point it would be relatively easy to install members in the courts. But how do you get around upholding the Constitution?

Lawyer: We support the Constitution—for the plebs. But we push through an Amendment that sets the Committee apart.

Director: You think people would vote for such an Amendment?

Lawyer: If times are dire and we offer hope? Yes, I do.

Director: So you'd be given supra-Constitutional powers.

Lawyer: In order to support the Constitution for the people, yes.

Director: But you live by no law other than aristocratic will. Haven't you heard the popular saying that no one is above the law?

Lawyer: And no one in their democratic regime would be above the law.

Director: But the Committee of Oversight would.

Lawyer: No, the Amendment would be our law.

Director: So that's the seam in the fabric of your aristocratic state.

Lawyer: Nothing is perfect. I think we can live with this.

Director: So you can't subvert the Constitution when it comes to others, but you aren't subject to it, except for your Amendment, yourselves.

Lawyer: Yes.

Director: It will never work.

Lawyer: Why not?

Director: You'll be like a foreign ruling class. You will be other.

Lawyer: That's the whole point!

Director: But who wants to be ruled by others?

Lawyer: Our rule will only gradually grow.

Director: How will it grow?

Lawyer: We'll go from oversight to assistance to management to rule.

Director: You're talking about your work with the people's elected officials.

Lawyer: I am. They will grow dependent on us to the point where we rule them.

Director: According to fact rather than law.

Lawyer: Yes, and who knows? Maybe one day we'll cement it in law. But the facts of the power structure will remain whether we do or not.

Director: So the nobles will rule two groups—themselves and those who rule the plebs. Are you sure you want no direct rule over plebs?

Lawyer: There will have to be extraordinary means for extraordinary occasions, but yes—no direct rule over plebs.

Director: Afraid you'll sully your hands?

Lawyer: You know better than that. It's best for the plebs not to have much contact with us. That, in turn, is good for us. You know, this is the most I've talked about aristocracy before. I need to work through some of my inconsistencies. We should talk about it again.

Director: I thought we had the night.

Lawyer: We do. I just have a lot to digest.

33

Director: What's the hardest thing to stomach?

Lawyer: The practical necessities of it all.

Director: Such as?

Lawyer: Being known as The Committee. I had somehow imagined something... grander.

Director: Well, thought impregnated your imagination and give birth to something more practical. Or isn't that how it seems to you?

Lawyer: No, that is how it seems to me. This is going to be a lot of work.

Director: More work than what you do now, that's for sure. Though your current work is probably good training. Still, you'll have to rely on the democracy coming to dire straits.

Lawyer: I refuse to contribute to that. A man of excellence can do no less.

Director: Would you actively work to support the democracy? To steer it clear of trouble?

Lawyer: What would you think of me if I said no?

Director: I'd say what you wish and what you do are one.

Lawyer: Would they be one if I worked against the democracy?

Director: Perhaps even more so. But then you're a sort of subversive. Is that what you want to be?

Lawyer: No, it's not. Subversives are men of questionable character. I want to come out of all of this with my character intact.

Director: So here's the scenario you depend upon. Things get bad. You're called on to help. You do in fact help. But to be able to guarantee your help in future times, you need a permanent footing. This permanent footing establishes you, in effect, as an aristocrat, along with your peers. Things go from there and your position is rendered permanent and secure. Does that sound about right?

Lawyer: Yes, that's about right.

Director: It's an old story. You'll really be doing nothing new. Did you want to be doing something new?

Lawyer: The story you articulate is usually the path of tyrants. We will be doing something new. We will be bringing excellence to the land. That's why we're taking no shortcuts on our journey there. We will arrive with our integrity intact.

Director: That would indeed be something new under the sun. Forgive me if I have my doubts. New things alarm.

Lawyer: Ha! It's not the fact of what we want to accomplish. It's the newness that alarms!

Director: I'm not so easily spooked by facts. But we have to wonder what might go wrong.

Lawyer: Well, as I said, aristocracies are fragile.

Director: Yes, didn't you mention training from youth and war as the keys?

Lawyer: They are the keys.

Director: I can see The Committee training its youth—possibly with the odd philosopher there to keep things honest. But war? Will you still be in charge of the troops? Isn't the president in charge? Or is that part of the Amendment?

Lawyer: I think it would have to be. If the president commands the troops, or the plebs somehow command—it's all over. They'll eventually sap us of our strength.

Director: You mean they'll take back their money.

Lawyer: Yes, that's what they'll do. And then it's back to the law firm for me and my descendants.

Director: But I thought we agreed the law firm isn't so bad.

Lawyer: It's bad because I know there's better.

Director: Not having to work for a living.

Lawyer: To put it baldly, yes.

Director: Is it possible—possible—that excellence is just an excuse for no work?

Lawyer: No! You have to work at being excellent, work harder than ever before.

Director: Okay, sorry. I had to ask. But now you seem to be justifying aristocracy with work.

34

Lawyer: Excellence is not about work. Work is required. But it in no way justifies aristocracy. Excellence itself justifies aristocracy.

Director: How tall can one of your descendants grow under the roof of The Committee?

Lawyer: It's a problem, as you suggest. Aristocrats need to be free. Eventually, as things straighten out, my descendants will be free.

Director: And what of you? Is it too late?

Lawyer: It's much too late. I received a democratic education from youth on up.

Director: Then it's a testament to you that you still love excellence. But don't democrats love excellence? Don't they have greatness in athletics, music, art, politics, business, and war?

Lawyer: It's true. But excellence is easy to love.

Director: What makes aristocrats different? Is it the money and freedom that it brings?

Lawyer: That's the sine qua non. You need a certain amount of freedom to develop your character traits. I'm not talking about the freedom to pursue the

American Dream. That's a freedom to stunt your development through excessive work for gain.

Director: Some dreamers don't work for gain. They work for the sake of the work. A doctor, say. She doesn't want to be famous. She just loves the work. Excellent, no?

Lawyer: It's hard to argue with that.

Director: Is she a natural aristocrat stuck in a democratic regime?

Lawyer: Is she happy?

Director: What if she is?

Lawyer: Is she satisfied?

Director: I don't know.

Lawyer: What would it take to know?

Director: I'd have to talk to her, get a sense of where she's at.

Lawyer: How do you get a sense of where someone is at?

Director: You look for longing. I see that longing in you, so I know you're not satisfied. You want something more. You want to live a life of excellence. I'd ask her something like this. But I think the question might not make sense to her.

Lawyer: And if it doesn't?

Director: She may already be living that excellent life.

Lawyer: But if she longs?

Director: Longing and happiness are opposed.

Lawyer: Yes. I've never heard it so clearly stated. The happy don't long; those who long aren't happy.

Director: If longing is nobler than happiness, should we long away our whole lives?

Lawyer: Well, 'long away' sounds like a waste of time. Longing for something good can bring you closer to that something good. This is progress and is... good.

Director: The progress brings you satisfaction.

Lawyer: Yes.

Director: Are you sure you want to maintain the distinction between happiness and satisfaction?

Lawyer: It's not up to what I want, Director. The distinction reflects the truth.

Director: But if I'm happy with a simple life, and I'm happy all day long—won't I retire at night satisfied with my lot?

Lawyer: Well....

Director: What's wrong?

Lawyer: You happiness depends on luck.

Director: Why do you say that?

Lawyer: Happy all day long? It means nothing comes crashing into your life to turn things upside down. The kind of satisfaction I'm talking about is within our control.

35

Director: Control. Is that what this is all about? Is excellence control?

Lawyer: Mastering your circumstances—achieving control—allows you to be satisfied.

Director: Can we ever really achieve control?

Lawyer: Not complete control, no. Not total control. But enough, enough to let us achieve our own degree of excellence.

Director: Our own degree. So there is no absolute excellence.

Lawyer: No, there isn't. People can set a high mark, but that's about it.

Director: Is excellence always a sort of competition?

Lawyer: Even if only competing with ourselves.

Director: Democrats compete, fiercely at times.

Lawyer: True. But they have to—have to—grub for money. Even if they are noble at heart and install themselves in a low paying job—the grubbing is there. There's no way around it. You need independent means if your competition is to be free.

Director: Free competition, that's the thing?

Lawyer: That's the only thing.

Director: So it's a life of striving.

Lawyer: Striving, yes.

Director: Why not be a life of... no striving?

Lawyer: No striving? Then what?

Director: Enjoyment of your means. Imagine a day where you rise, take a walk, have your breakfast, take care of your affairs, have lunch, read a book, meet with friends, have tea, go for another walk, have dinner, see a show, read for a while, and go to bed.

Lawyer: That sounds nice—for a day.

Director: It's not enough for you?

Lawyer: I need to rule. And we described what a day like that would be before.

Director: So as a member of The Committee, you would review the overall state's affairs; you would discuss them with peers; then you would act.

Lawyer: And that activity of rule would inform the rest of my day. It would provide fodder for my thoughts. It would determine what I choose to read—maybe even what I choose to write.

Director: Ah, you have ambitions as an author?

Lawyer: I'm not sure 'ambition' is the right word. I look at it this way. Who better to write than someone present at the creation?

Director: The creation of the aristocracy. Well, you have a point. But we've been bouncing between needing centuries or longer to needing The Committee during our lifetimes. Which will it be?

Lawyer: I honestly don't know. If it's during my lifetime, I will be ready. If later, much later, I'll help pave the way.

Director: Through friendships and possibly writings.

Lawyer: Yes. Friends and writings are key.

Director: Would you be content if no one knew about The Committee's aristocratic nature other than those of The Committee?

Lawyer: Living the life is all that counts. But then there's more reason to write. We'd ensure that future generations know the truth, that we were more than some addition built onto a fundamentally democratic state.

Director: I understand why the farce is necessary at first. But over time? Will The Committee simply become the state?

Lawyer: But it's no farce. Remember what we said? It's necessary.

Director: And when The Committee is no longer necessary?

Lawyer: It will always be necessary—more so, even, as time goes on. When it reaches total necessity we drop the name Committee and call it the state.

Director: The few governing the many in broad daylight, the aristocrat's dream made true.

Lawyer: It really is a journey to the light.

Director: Why, do you feel like you live under a rock now? Rich, well connected, a power in our city.

Lawyer: I don't live under a rock. I would never live under a rock even in the worst circumstances we can imagine. That's not me.

Director: But still, you'd like more light.

Lawyer: I want to be free to be me. I am an aristocrat at heart. Why? I don't know. But I know that's what I am. It's always appealed to me since I was a kid. What appealed to you?

Director: Philosophy from the start.

Lawyer: What was that start like?

Director: I listened to the adults around me and found they didn't agree. I asked them why and got strange answers. These answers puzzled me. So I asked more questions. And more questions. Until I got good at asking questions.

Lawyer: Were the adults annoyed?

Director: Some were. Some smiled and sent me away. One, an older cousin, bought me a book.

Lawyer: What was it?

Director: Plato's collected works.

Lawyer: Did you read it?

Director: Many times.

Lawyer: Did it help?

Director: It helped me get better at asking questions.

Lawyer: You understood the book?

Director: No. But I know what I didn't understand. So I set out to learn.

Lawyer: That sounds very much like a life of excellence to me.

Director: I don't know. I just knew I had questions and I was going to find out.

Lawyer: Did you find out?

Director: Some things. Some things I still don't know. But over time my questions changed.

Lawyer: What do you question now?

Director: Why a man with a golden place in our current regime wants to see that regime overthrown.

Lawyer: Because I want something more. You have your questions. I have this.

Director: What don't you like about our current regime?

Lawyer: All the overachievers.

Director: What? Says someone who promotes a life of striving for excellence.

Lawyer: You need a natural degree of ability—an abundance, actually—if you are to succeed as an aristocrat. In our regime so many mediocre people strive to get ahead. The sight of it sickens me.

Director: How do you know they're mediocre?

Lawyer: Oh, you can just tell, can't you? There's nothing original in them. They mimic others in everything they do. Watch the business world in particular. They follow each other in a herd. Certain buzz words gain currency and that's all they can talk about. Certain management gurus come into vogue and everyone learns to think like them.

Director: Is that your real problem?

Lawyer: No. It's that they're shameless in all this. They have no shame! They just want to get ahead. They don't care what it takes.

Director: But you care. You have shame.

Lawyer: Of course I care! And I do have shame. Anyone who loves excellence has a sense of shame. You want to live up to your own standards. The mediocre in business have no standard except the bottom line.

Director: Some would say even the exceptional in business have no standard but the bottom line.

Lawyer: I'm sure that's so for many. But I know a few who are very successful who do have a standard beyond the bottom line.

Director: Yes, but I've heard people like this speak. They all say the same thing. If you follow your standard—it will ultimately improve the bottom line. In other words, they justify their standard by the bottom line.

37

Lawyer: You know, I'm not willing to win at all costs. I've lost a few cases because of this.

Director: You've kept your integrity.

Lawyer: I have.

Director: What did your clients say? Did they know you could have done more?

Lawyer: The ones who lost? I told them situation. They agreed with me.

Director: Then you were very lucky. Not everyone would.

Lawyer: No, definitely not. In a way, those cases were the luckiest days of my career. They earned me true friends.

Director: Yes, but no one likes to lose.

Lawyer: True, but I won with them later in different things. It helped make up for the loss.

Director: They trusted you to come through—and you did. Are these friends aristocrats at heart?

Lawyer: They are.

Director: Could you tell because of the way they handled the loss?

Lawyer: Yes. They are people of integrity. They wouldn't have it any other way.

Director: I know democrats who are people of integrity. Don't you?

Lawyer: I do. And you want to know what makes them different? They think most people have integrity, too—it's just the bad ones who don't. I don't believe that.

Director: You think only the few have integrity.

Lawyer: Yes, and I'm not talking about for everyday things. I'm talking about when push comes to shove. Where do you stand on this?

Director: Very few have true integrity.

Lawyer: I knew that's what you thought! But are you suggesting there are few within the few?

Director: I don't know, Lawyer. I've never spent time in an aristocracy, let alone one like yours. But something tells me that human nature doesn't change.

Lawyer: Do you think it's some sort of group dynamic thing? Within a given group there will always be few of true integrity?

Director: I honestly don't know. Maybe under optimal conditions integrity will flourish. Maybe you're going to create the optimal conditions. But....

Lawyer: You're concerned with the problem of evil.

Director: Can you say more?

Lawyer: Does evil go away with excellent social engineering? That's a question I have. But I'm aware an affirmative answer raises questions of free will.

Director: Do you care if you have free will, whatever that is, if you have the best regime?

Lawyer: Honestly? No. If I could have excellence I'd be willing to trade in my choice.

Director: But isn't excellence the art of making good choices?

Lawyer: You have a point. Maybe the question doesn't matter. Like you said—free will, whatever that is. But I am still concerned about the few within the few. If that's how it works out, we're in for trouble.

Director: Maybe you should plan for the worst and hope for the best. Assume few aristocrats will have full integrity. What does that mean for the state?

Lawyer: Only those with full integrity must rule in the ultimate sense. Yes, all aristocrats will rule. No, not all of them will hold positions of importance.

Director: How do you guarantee the right people are in?

Lawyer: It's going to take some luck. The nominating committee for positions of trust must be comprised, from the start, of excellent souls. If we can start out right, we can hope for much.

Director: It takes one to know one?

Lawyer: It's not so much that as it's that it takes one to promote one. We won't put cronies in place. We'll only go with true hearts.

38

Director: Maybe there's a way help along luck?

Lawyer: Here's the problem. At the time, we're not going to know who's heart is true or not. They'll all seem true. That's why they'll be on The Committee.

Director: How large will this committee be?

Lawyer: I don't know. I suppose circumstances will have a way of forcing an answer on us.

Director: What if your friends refuse to be forced?

Lawyer: Poor decisions will be made. And we'll ruin the regime—the one chance in history for such a regime.

Director: Hmm.

Lawyer: Hmm what?

Director: I've noticed that those of the highest integrity don't always know what's best.

Lawyer: Why not?

Director: They're not as flexible as they might be.

Lawyer: So I have to gather those with both integrity and flexibility.

Director: If you want things to turn out well, yes.

Lawyer: How do I do this?

Director: I have no idea. Maybe you rely only on yourself?

Lawyer: I set up the regime?

Director: That's what Lycurgus did in Sparta. One man alone.

Lawyer: Yes, but that story comes to us through the mists of ancient history. Who knows what really went on?

Director: So you're not aiming to be famous through the mists of history?

Lawyer: I'm really not looking for fame. I want to live a good life. If that brings fame, so be it. But I'm not angling for that.

Director: That might make your judgment more sound when it comes to important things. The would-be famous are often blind. All they can see is themselves.

Lawyer: I need to distinguish natural aristocrats from those born to live under other sorts of rule.

Director: Should we look to how they were raised?

Lawyer: Their parents? Yes, but I know aristocrats who come from not the best homes. It's just something given in a person's life, a given of origin unknown.

Director: They're chosen.

Lawyer: Yes, and there's no easy way to know who those people are. Sometimes we live through difficult experiences and learn their identity. Once we know, we hold on to them for dear life. We work with them to found a regime, where others like them are welcome.

Director: Hold on. I thought this was going to be a hereditary aristocracy based on a certain amount of annual tax proceeds. How many of these people do you think you'll let in?

Lawyer: Ha! Do you imagine there are so many of them we'll have trouble here?

Director: If there aren't, how will you have enough people to found your regime? Too bad your base can't be global. You might be more likely to find more noble souls.

Lawyer: That would make the problem of establishing The Committee that much harder. Americans aren't going to grant oversight to foreigners.

Director: Then Americans only it is. You'll just have to make do. But this raises a sort of thorny question.

Lawyer: Oh? What?

Director: Are you a patriot? Or rather, will you be a patriot? Sorry, I just had to ask.

Lawyer: You're right to question here. What is patriotism?

Director: Love of country. Do you love this country?

Lawyer: Yes, I do.

Director: And yet you want to bring about a change of regime.

Lawyer: The two aren't mutually exclusive.

Director: You'd better explain.

39

Lawyer: I don't love regimes. I love the people and the place.

Director: You mean the physical place?

Lawyer: Yes, the soil; the rivers; the lakes; the mountains; the deserts—all of this stuff. It is my own. I was born here to this land.

Director: And you love the people?

Lawyer: I love the people I know and love, not all of the people.

Director: But there might be others among the people you might come to know and love?

Lawyer: Sure. Chance might bring us together.

Director: Or you could search them out. Haven't you ever admired someone you read about?

Lawyer: Yes, but we only know the truth in person.

Director: I disagree. I have a friend who is painfully shy. You can barely get to know him in person. But you should read his books! You get to know who he really is.

Lawyer: Point taken. I'll make a point to search out more and more good books written in our land. And I suppose that will make me even more of a patriot! I just don't care for our regime.

Director: So you would undertake to make a fundamental change in how we live our lives.

Lawyer: Life won't change that much for most. And there is a good chance we will create, for the worthy few, the most wonderful place on Earth. Ask me if I'm a patriot then. Better still, ask me now.

Director: Are you a patriot of this place?

Lawyer: I love this place like a mother who is about to give birth to a wonderful child—our aristocracy.

Director: So, what? Are you the mother democracy, our amazing democracy that births the few?

Lawyer: Oh, what does it matter? Patriotism is the last refuge of a scoundrel.

Director: I thought you were going to say patriotism is the virtue of the vicious.

Lawyer: It's basically the very same thought. Ask me something more concrete. Would I fight for our country? I already have. I've killed and bled in its name. I know you have, too. I think that qualifies us as patriots, Director. Don't you?

Director: We fought for the ones beside us. No?

Lawyer: We did.

Director: That's all anyone would do.

Lawyer: Look, you know I'm not one to take credit for actions in war. Those actions have their own truth. Some of that truth is beautiful; some of it is ugly. That's how I think it is with all patriotic deeds. But will you damn me for wanting a better way?

Director: A better way is a better way. But let me ask you one thing. Please don't force a better way. If a better way appears, take it. But don't ram it down our throats.

Lawyer: I don't think I even have a choice! Who am I to ram anything down anyone's throat? Even if I wanted to, circumstances wouldn't allow. If the democracy is strong, no ramming is possible. If it's weak, there's no need to ram—it will be looking for help.

Director: Well, that's a relief. You are really democracy's helper in the guise of an aristocrat. In fact, the whole aristocracy exists in order to bail poor democracy out! A perfect symbiotic relationship.

Lawyer: Make no mistake, Director. I believe the democracy will eventually wither, leaving the aristocracy intact. Will this take centuries? Probably, unless we live through catastrophic events. And be certain about this. I would never seek to bring about catastrophe in order to achieve my ends.

40

Director: Yes, I never thought of you as the heartless, ruthless type you sometimes would seem to be. But I do think you're willing to turn a blind eye from time to time. Will you keep company with those who plot catastrophe?

Lawyer: No.

Director: But you're willing to take advantage of what they work.

Lawyer: If they create a catastrophe, I will act in the way I see fit, given the circumstances.

Director: No doubt you will. As would I.

Lawyer: As should we all.

Director: Yes. And the democrats will see fit to do this; and the aristocrats will see fit to do that.

Lawyer: And the philosophers? What will they see fit to do? Which faction will they support?

Director: I have no idea. It depends on so many things.

Lawyer: What kind of things?

Director: Where they find themselves, for one.

Lawyer: Are you saying their support is based on circumstances?

Director: What isn't based on circumstances? Or are you going to tell me you're an absolutist?

Lawyer: I'm not. I take your point. Sometimes our side is chosen for us. There can be good people on either side.

Director: Sometimes there are more than two sides.

Lawyer: Of course.

Director: Do you think someone's religion has anything to do with it? I mean, does a certain religion, or lack of religion, predispose someone one way or another?

Lawyer: I don't know. I've never really thought about it. What do you think?

Director: One thing comes to mind. The soul. If the religion believes in an individual soul, and that this soul is equal to all other souls in the eyes of God, that lends a certain support to democracy, where all are individuals and equal before the law.

Lawyer: What religion supports aristocracy?

Director: Hmm. I'm not sure. I don't know enough about the various religions. But it would stand to reason that if there were different types of souls....

Lawyer: I find that hard even to think.

Director: Yes, it cuts against our grain. But maybe there's a seed that can be exploited.

Lawyer: What seed?

Director: In at least one of our major religions, some souls are saved and some souls are damned. Two different types of soul?

Lawyer: Maybe. But I see your point. Still, I don't know that I'd want to damn all the plebs.

Director: Nor save all the nobles. Maybe religion doesn't matter here.

Lawyer: But I think you're on to something important. The plebs will lead a hard life. Hard life leads to religion. This religion might undermine the regime. We have to get ahead of this, Director.

Director: How can we get ahead of it if we don't know what it is?

Lawyer: Maybe their lives shouldn't be so hard. Maybe we have to take it easy on them so that no subversive religion takes root.

Director: From what we were saying before, these people are going to live much like they live today. Is life so hard here?

Lawyer: I think it is. But people are too proud to complain.

Director: Where do they get their pride?

Lawyer: They are equal and free.

Director: You would take both of those things away from them.

Lawyer: So you think they'd be likely to complain?

Director: Yes.

41

Lawyer: Their pride would have to be broken by calamity before we could establish the aristocracy. They would have to be willing to grant us power.

Director: It's going to take some calamity.

Lawyer: I think we're headed that way, don't you?

Director: This country is in the business of reinventing itself every so often. Each time it does a certain segment of the population loses, and another segment wins. Calamity to the former, opportunity to the latter.

Lawyer: How do we break the cycle?

Director: You'd have to solidify things.

Lawyer: How?

Director: Make the regime less flexible. Tighten up your interpretation of the Constitution.

Lawyer: It does come down to lawyers, doesn't?

Director: They play a major role.

Lawyer: But what are we saying? Conservatives will destroy the regime?

Director: That's how it looks to me. So if you want to save the regime, become a progressive.

Lawyer: I am thoroughly confused!

Director: Yes, you said you were some sort of progressive. I can see how that might be confusing.

Lawyer: My progressive efforts to introduce an aristocracy will help save the democratic regime. That's actually... funny!

Director: I'm glad you can see that.

Lawyer: So in humoring me you're actually hoping to save democracy?

Director: I've been accused of worse.

Lawyer: Ha! I don't believe you. I don't think you really have any political hopes.

Director: What hopes do you think I have?

Lawyer: Strictly personal hopes, for you and your friends.

Director: Alright, you've got me, Lawyer. I do have hopes for you. I hope that you'll find satisfaction in what you do.

Lawyer: And if that involves establishing an aristocracy?

Director: Then it involves establishing an aristocracy. And if you realize you've made a mistake, I hope you'll find satisfaction in correcting what you've done.

Lawyer: How could someone possibly correct the mistake of founding a regime?

Director: I'm sure if we look closely enough we'll find an example of that in the founding of the current regime. Surely one of the fathers suffered a bout of conscience at one point or another.

Lawyer: That never occurred to me. But I bet you're right. They not only broke with an aristocracy; they broke with an aristocratic way of life.

Director: Well, they did maintain a certain lifestyle. But yes, they broke with a way of life.

Lawyer: I want to break with a democratic way of life.

Director: You're on your way. Do you think you'll suffer from bouts of conscience?

Lawyer: I do, truth be told. It's a good thing the change will be gradual. I mean, with the founding of the current regime people lived in a more or less democratic fashion, isolated from the motherland, for more than a hundred years before the revolution took place.

Director: Maybe you're at the start of the hundred.

Lawyer: Yes, but there have always been aristocratically minded people in America. Maybe we're at the end of the hundred.

Director: Who can say these things with certainty? Just follow your heart and see where it leads.

42

Lawyer: As if where it leads might not be extremely dangerous!

Director: Play with fire and you might get burned. You know that.

Lawyer: That's why you don't play?

Director: I don't play because these things are complicated, and I need to look before I leap.

Lawyer: You're just looking for the main chance. You're an opportunist.

Director: And you're a principled aristocrat? I'm sensible, not an opportunist. I'm not trying to get ahead.

Lawyer: No, you're just trying to do the right thing. Which means you're trying to play it safe.

Director: Then will you be so bold to speak with others what you've spoken to me?

Lawyer: When the time is right, yes. I just might not speak openly about aristocracy. I'll talk about the need for The Committee, and so on. It will be for a long time an aristocracy in everything but name. Just as it's a plutocracy in everything but name today.

Director: The rule of the wealthy. The wealthy always seem to have their say, except under extraordinary circumstances. Are you sure you wouldn't like to become exceedingly rich rather than an aristocrat?

Lawyer: I want to become an aristocrat for my descendants' sake. I want them to inherit a life allowing for excellence.

Director: And what about you?

Lawyer: I'm a transitional figure. And maybe many of my line will be, too. We'll have hope for the future.

Director: The psychology of this is elusive. You'll live in hope that the democracy will fail? Won't that make you resentful of the democracy's successes?

Lawyer: The psychology is no doubt complex. But I don't want to become resentful, bitter. Aristocrats shouldn't be bitter.

Director: What should they be?

Lawyer: Healthy in every sense. The healthy aren't bitter. The healthy are satisfied.

Director: But if satisfied perhaps not striving for excellence? Don't we have to be dissatisfied in order to strive?

Lawyer: You have a point. This is the tension in the soul of the aristocrat—to be satisfied and dissatisfied at once.

Director: An aristocrat always wants more.

Lawyer: We all want more. But only some of us do something about it.

Director: Plutocrats want more money; they do something about it. Democrats want more equality; they do something about it. Aristocrats want more excellence; what do they do about it?

Lawyer: Do you have any idea how hard it is to rule? Aristocrats want to be better at rule. They strive for this with all their might.

Director: What does rule entail?

Lawyer: You have to command the facts and you have to be persuasive.

Director: That's it? That's all it takes to rule? I can command the facts. I've been known to be persuasive. Does that mean I rule?

Lawyer: Maybe it does.

Director: But what do I persuade towards? What am I trying to do with my persuasion? What would an aristocrat do?

Lawyer: A ruler—a statesman, I should say—steers the ship of state through storms. To come out of the storm intact takes very great skill.

Director: I don't doubt that. But why not rule in a democracy? Democracies go through storms. Statesmen lead them out.

Lawyer: True, but democratic statesmen have to compromise themselves. They have to pretend to be of the people themselves.

Director: What if they are of the people? Or is the point that you, you're not of the people, my friend? The circles you move in are elite. Are you saying you wouldn't pretend to be other than you are?

Lawyer: That's exactly what I'm saying. I must be what I am.

Director: You're an elitist. And aristocracy is the form of government elitists prefer.

Lawyer: You make it sound so simple and bad. But I am an elitist. That's for sure.

Director: In a democracy elitist is a dirty word. The elite are thought to be bankrupt frauds. How can someone be better than someone else?

Lawyer: You think I haven't heard it all before? Pit one of my elite in government against a simple soul of the people and see who saves the ship.

Director: If you save the ship, people will recognize your right to rule? That's ironic, no? In recognizing your right to rule they would subvert the democracy, the thing you'll save. Or is there something more going on here?

Lawyer: What do you mean?

Director: What are you really saving? The democracy? Or something else?

Lawyer: Yes, I think I know what you mean. I'd be saving people, not The People. People have an existence beyond their regimes. Or should I say beneath their regimes? Either way, you have an excellent point.

Director: A neighbor is a neighbor despite his politics. Just because you have many neighbors doesn't mean you're a man of the people in the democratic sense. Kings have many subjects.

Lawyer: Yes, I know exactly what you mean. And sometimes they say of kings they are for the people. But usually that means they are against the aristocrats.

Director: Are aristocrats ever for the people?

Lawyer: Maybe individual aristocrats can be, which pits them against their peers. But as a whole? Can an aristocracy be pro people? I don't know. I'm not sure it's ever been done.

Director: Why not? What difficulty is there here?

Lawyer: It has to do with the basic assumption of aristocracy—that few are capable of living an excellent life. Maybe there is the odd person of the people who can, and we've talked about making provision for this. But can most of the many be like the few? The answer has to be no, or the regime must fall.

Director: That's what's peculiar about aristocracy. Even a plutocracy can be pro people. You can be in favor of the people and not give your money away. But if an aristocrat is in favor of the people he is at odds with his peers. It's the peers that cause the trouble.

Lawyer: Of course. But I'm not sure about your plutocrat. To be in favor of the people must mean something. It can't just be an empty wish. What can it be but to give money to them? In doing that, the plutocrat abandons his peers.

Director: Unless they follow suit.

Lawyer: You will never get a majority of plutocrats to follow suit. They love their money too much.

Director: And aristocrats love their excellence too much. But what stops a whole people from loving excellence?

Lawyer: Oh, Director. You probably know human nature better than I. You should answer your own question.

Director: There's much to go wrong in life. Some of it is our fault; much of it is not. When things go wrong excellence is usually lost. And in a whole people, a lot can go wrong. But aristocrats are experts at limiting what can go wrong. That's why they have the life you describe.

Lawyer: Yes, and given all that they ought to feel shame if they falter or fail.

Director: Shame is so important to the aristocratic psyche. Does that bother you?

Lawyer: Not in the least. It's an excellent check. It's an excellent spur. A shamed aristocrat is a disgraced aristocrat.

Director: Yes, but it doesn't do to have too many of them around. They'll stir up trouble.

Lawyer: Yes, they certainly will. So how do we prevent that from happening?

Director: I don't know. You won't want to lower your standards. Maybe if someone is shamed enough you have to banish him from the realm.

Lawyer: Yes, the shamed are like a cancer in the state. I think we have to be ruthless here.

44

Director: And if you're ruthless to your own, you ought to have no trouble being ruthless to others. It's a good psychological anchor.

Lawyer: It's called integrity. We treat ourselves the same as we treat others.

Director: I don't know if it's called integrity. It might just be good policy. And isn't that really what's at the heart of your regime?

Lawyer: Good policy? Maybe. But do you know how hard it is to implement good policy once you've thought it up?

Director: I'm not sure it works that way. I think people find their limits and then decide on a policy that accommodates them. It's not that they arrive at some perfect policy then measure themselves against it.

Lawyer: I don't know, Director. Sometimes it's clear what needs to be done, but we know we don't have what it takes to do it.

Director: You have a point. Will that be a problem in your regime?

Lawyer: If it ever becomes a problem we can't solve, the regime is at an end.

Director: What happens when aristocracies cease?

Lawyer: There is usually a backlash against the aristocrats by the plebs—unless a dictator, or king, or emperor can keep the internal peace.

Director: So the few would favor the rule of one when they come to dire straits. And this one would protect the few but favor the many.

Lawyer: That's how it would work.

Director: Wouldn't the few rather go out in a blaze of glory than settle for protection from some king?

Lawyer: I certainly would. But here's the problem. Those with that preference are gone. That's why the regime falls into dire straits.

Director: That can't be right. Those with that preference are sometimes, often hot-headed. They make many mistakes. Hot-heads aren't statesmen, right? So it can't be that preference alone.

Lawyer: You're right. That preference must come with excellent judgment.

Director: When is it excellent to judge it's best to go out in a blaze?

Lawyer: When the only alternative is intolerable.

Director: You're saying you'd have no choice. But is it a mark of excellence to simply do what you must do?

Lawyer: Of course it is! How many people don't do what they must do? They hem and they haw; they try half-measures; they do anything but the needful. That's the rule, Director. Going out in a blaze is always the exception.

Director: Is this going out a sort of suicide?

Lawyer: You can call it that if you like. But most suicides are pathetic, not glorious.

Director: So you're talking about dying in battle.

Lawyer: Yes. There's all the difference in the world between dying in battle and committing a lonely act.

Director: What is that difference?

Lawyer: Pride.

Director: Oh, I don't know. Many a Roman suicide died with pride.

Lawyer: And many of them probably died with shame.

Director: Maybe in their shame they recaptured their pride through death.

Lawyer: Maybe. But suicide isn't the point. The point is not being willing to live a certain fallen life.

Director: What do you call those who fall but carry on?

Lawyer: Cowards.

Director: But isn't it very difficult to carry on after a fall? Isn't that one of the most difficult things in the world?

Lawyer: Difficulty alone doesn't make something good.

Director: What makes something good?

Lawyer: That's a very difficult question. But I have a simple answer. To rule well is good.

45

Director: So all things associated with ruling well are good?

Lawyer: I want to say yes. What does it mean to rule well? To protect the regime that allows for excellence.

Director: Which is to say to protect the regime that allows one to rule well. To protect in order to be able to protect.

Lawyer: It has a certain neatness, don't you think?

Director: Who can argue with that? It's a perpetual motion machine.

Lawyer: Those are the only kinds of governments that work.

Director: What sets democracy in motion?

Lawyer: Our democracy is set in motion by the American Dream.

Director: Do you think other democracies had their dreams?

Lawyer: I don't know. But I think it's a good question. I'd like to see a historian's findings on this. Maybe democracy has to have a dream. If it doesn't, it consumes itself.

Director: Do aristocrats and kings need a dream?

Lawyer: I can't speak for kings. But aristocrats are living the dream.

Director: The dream of ruling well. And I suppose that if they fail to live the dream, they fail to be aristocrats at all.

Lawyer: Yes, the regime will collapse. Live the dream or die.

Director: Do democrats have to live the dream or die—those that have a dream, of course?

Lawyer: In a sense. But they can go on not living the dream. An aristocrat can't.

Director: If many democrats don't live the dream, a majority, doesn't the regime collapse?

Lawyer: I don't know that a majority ever lives the dream.

Director: How many do you think do?

Lawyer: Let me correct myself. Maybe there was a time when the majority lived the dream, or at least enough of it to live tolerably well. And maybe that's all the dream is—to live tolerably well. If so, then I'd say that a majority must live tolerably well or there is hell to pay.

Director: Tolerably well is an awfully low bar. Can't we say people need to live well? You rule well; the people live well.

Lawyer: Are you suggesting aristocrats don't live well?

Director: If you're so bent on ruling, it's possible you won't. There's more to life than rule.

Lawyer: Tell the democratic dreamers that there's more to life than work. But rule is such an all-encompassing thing. Rule shapes how we live our lives. To say you rule is to say much, very much.

Director: Is it to say much in democratic rule?

Lawyer: Democrats are limited in how they can rule.

Director: And aristocrats aren't? After all, they have their peers to consider— peers who want to rule, not be ruled. How will you handle being ruled in your state?

Lawyer: We will rule and be ruled in turn. Yes, that sets a limit on rule. But we will willingly obey good rule. Democrats aren't always good at this.

Director: I'm sure you'll be much better. But who decides what rule is good? You'll have a society of equals, your peers. Yes, some will hold higher positions and ranks; but you're suggesting this will only be for a time. All will take part in rule. And all will feel fully entitled to judge.

Lawyer: Democrats feel fully entitled to judge—even when they don't deserve a hearing. Any fool can vote. Any fool can run his mouth in praise or blame.

Director: Won't it be the same in the aristocracy?

Lawyer: You're less likely to talk like a fool if you've had to bear the burden of rule yourself. That's the big difference here. And let's not forget the training from earliest youth on up. All will be trained in the science and art of rule.

46

Director: There's a science of rule?

Lawyer: Oh, don't play dumb. Philosophers and historians have taught this science since ancient times. You've read most of them.

Director: Rule concerns human nature. You're saying there's a science to human nature. To me it's not always that clear.

Lawyer: I think it will become more clear when everyone strives toward knowledge of this. Can you imagine what it would be like to grow up in such company?

Director: It is indeed hard to imagine. Wonderful, but hard. What will you do about those who believe they know?

Lawyer: But don't? We certainly won't coddle them. People will be damned sure they know before they speak.

Director: Are you worried that might stifle thought?

Lawyer: The opposite will occur. People will think because they want to know.

Director: You mean people will think because they want to speak.

Lawyer: Is there anything wrong with that? If there is anything that encourages thought, isn't that thing good?

Director: Pain can encourage thought. Is pain then good?

Lawyer: Some pain is good. You know this, Director.

Director: Maybe what can come of the pain is good. About the pain itself I have my doubts.

Lawyer: Why do you doubt aristocracy?

Director: That's a big question. I'll answer with a little sentence. I fear the self-selection of the rulers.

Lawyer: Do you think democrats do such a better job? Don't they select themselves, meaning those like them?

Director: Sometimes they do; sometimes they don't. But I think more often they don't.

Lawyer: Why not?

Director: To appeal to the people you have to make them out to be better than they are. A true man of the people isn't gifted in this. He tends to speak to them as they are. But someone who is exceptional? Someone who feels himself to be other? He will make them out to be the best.

Lawyer: Why?

Director: Because he believes he is the best. Or rather, he suspects he is among the best. The people's belief in him is proof.

Lawyer: So he strives to win their belief in order to win belief in himself. That's his fundamental need. That's why he does what he does. Aristocrats have no need for this. They believe in themselves from birth.

Director: And that's what makes them dangerous.

Lawyer: Do you think self-doubt is good?

Director: If you're in the wrong, and come to doubt, I'd say that's good.

Lawyer: But everything will be arranged so that the few are in the right.

Director: Who decides what's right?

Lawyer: Who decides in a democracy? The people decide what's right.

Director: People who haven't been raised to think they're absolutely right.

Lawyer: Oh, you know better than that. Democrats believe theirs is the only true regime. They're taught this as an absolute truth from earliest youth on up. Every regime thinks this way.

Director: Hmm. You have a point. And I think every regime trains its ruling class to rule. You will teach the aristocrats. A monarch is taught, for sure. And democrats train their own.

Lawyer: How do they train them?

Director: They're taught that all are equal; that all have rights; that to lead you need to persuade, and leadership is consummated in the vote. These lessons are taught over and over again until they are part of one's nature—until one is prepared to rule.

Lawyer: But you yourself said the real statesmen in democracies are not men of the people, in an essential sense.

Director: Maybe the real statesmen in aristocracies are not men of the few.

47

Lawyer: You seem to want to blur the lines between aristocracy and democracy.

Director: It's not about what I want. I think there is one essential difference. The many support themselves in a democracy. The many support the few in an aristocracy. Am I missing something here?

Lawyer: You want to suggest that aristocrats cannot support themselves.

Director: I don't think it's a matter of cannot. I think it's a matter of will not. And who knows? Maybe eventually it becomes a matter of cannot.

Lawyer: Do you think democrats are more able than aristocrats?

Director: This raises the question of breeding. I suppose that's another essential difference, one I overlooked. Democrats can breed with whomever they like. Aristocrats can only breed within the few.

Lawyer: Are you going to argue that mutts are more intelligent than purebreds, and so on?

Director: No, I think certain traits carry—and it's not an entirely genetic thing. But will aristocrats breed for these traits, or will they breed for something else?

Lawyer: You mean good looks.

Director: Yes, that's a powerful factor in breeding.

Lawyer: Aristocrats in Europe looked different than the peasants. There was a type.

Director: Do you want to establish an aristocratic type here? It would make it easier, you know.

Lawyer: Would make what easier?

Director: To have contempt for the plebs. It's always easier to have contempt for those who look different than us.

Lawyer: I don't want that.

Director: You don't want to look different?

Lawyer: Honestly? I do. But I meant I don't want to feel contempt.

Director: Why not? Shared contempt is a very good social glue.

Lawyer: Contempt derives from arrogance; and arrogance leads to bad mistakes.

Director: In other words, it will be easier to rule the plebs if you don't have contempt.

Lawyer: Not easier. Nothing is easier than contempt. But the rule will be better without contempt. More true. Contempt brings on a sort of blindness. To rule you have to see. That's where philosophy comes in.

Director: Do you think philosophers can't have contempt?

Lawyer: Can they?

Director: Of course! Philosophers aren't morally perfect.

Lawyer: That's funny. I never stopped to consider that truth. Of course they're not morally perfect. They're human. But in their thinking are they free? If you, the man, feel contempt—does that necessarily bleed into your thought?

Director: That's a very difficult question. It has to do with what thought is. But I'd like to return to aristocracy. You spoke of inviting philosophers in. You have to be very careful what kind of philosophers you bring. Bring those with a predilection for contempt and you will have endless trouble here.

Lawyer: What sort should we bring? What sorts of vices should they have?

Director: Anything but the vices aristocrats commonly have. They will amplify those vices beyond all control.

Lawyer: So where do aristocratic leaning philosophers go?

Director: To democracies, where else?

Lawyer: So you think democratically minded philosophers should go to aristocracies?

Director: Yes, it's good for both the philosophers and their friends.

Lawyer: That somehow makes strange sense. But I like how you said friends rather that students.

Director: Teachers want students; philosophers want friends.

Lawyer: Why don't philosophers want students? I like what you're saying, but I don't understand why.

Director: Philosophers as philosophers have nothing to teach. They explore with their friends; they learn together.

Lawyer: Some would say that's what a good teacher does.

Director: Sure. But at the end of the day people expect teachers to teach. And in order to teach, you have to have knowledge the students lack.

48

Lawyer: Can't the same person be teacher and philosopher?

Director: Yes, certainly. At times you philosophize; at times you teach.

Lawyer: What would you teach?

Director: How to philosophize.

Lawyer: Is that something aristocrats need to know?

Director: As aristocrats? No. As human beings? Yes.

Lawyer: So you're saying aristocracy and human excellence don't go hand in hand?

Director: No, I think they can.

Lawyer: Then what are you saying?

Director: Aristocracy is the most anti-philosophical of all regimes. Therefore it is the regime that has most need of philosophy.

Lawyer: I'm stunned. The natural aristocrats I know all have a love for philosophy.

Director: They love philosophical books. I'm not sure they ever encountered a living philosopher.

Lawyer: What would happen if they did?

Director: Philosophy might lose its charm. Some people who read old philosophical books like to think those books support their tastes. And some of them do. But a living philosopher doesn't like to be a support.

Lawyer: Why not? What's wrong with being a support?

Director: Well, we have to ask what we're supporting. In this case, it's taste. Do tastes need support? To my mind we all have to fight for our own tastes. We need to stand on our own.

Lawyer: But isn't that what friends are? People who share common tastes?

Director: In large part, yes—certainly. But are they crutches to one another? Or are they independent souls who come together to celebrate their successes in living up to their tastes?

Lawyer: Well, when you put it like that I have to agree. Aristocracy really is a taste at heart.

Director: Can it be an acquired taste?

Lawyer: I don't think so. What do those people call it? A certain sense of life. You have it or you don't. It never changes.

Director: Do people know they have this sense of life?

Lawyer: What a strange question. But I think I understand why you ask. A person with an aristocratic sense of life living in a democracy might have that sense crushed. He wouldn't know what hit him. He might never come to see his taste for what it is. Confusion puts it mildly.

Director: Yes, it does. What a world we live in. It's as if cards of differing suits are shuffled and tossed around the planet. Then we have to play the hand we're given.

Lawyer: Oh, to have a flush. What I wouldn't give to be surrounded by my own.

Director: Poor you. And I'm being sincere. An aristocratic soul in a democracy.

Lawyer: Stop it. You know I'm not looking for pity.

Director: And I'm not offering it. I'm just stating the facts. And look how many lucky democrats there are!

Lawyer: They're happy like pigs in shit.

Director: That's taking it a bit far, but point taken.

Lawyer: Why is it too far?

Director: There are much worse regimes than democracy, my friend. Think of true mob rule. That's more what you were thinking.

Lawyer: True. But there's something more honest about mob rule. Democracy is the mob all dressed up in pretty clothes. What? You have nothing to say?

Director: Mob rule is a terror. Democracy is certainly imperfect, but do you really describe it as a cloaked terror?

Lawyer: Alright, maybe I'm being extreme. But there's something about the constant reduction to the lowest common denominator that frightens.

Director: What does that phrase about the lowest common denominator mean?

Lawyer: It means that nothing higher survives. Democracy kills the nobler growths.

49

Director: You don't think there are noble growths in democracy? Your existence argues against your point.

Lawyer: I don't consider that flattery. But do you have any idea how hard it is to always be against the grain?

Director: I can only imagine.

Lawyer: Ha! I shouldn't have asked. I got carried away. Philosophers don't have it easy, I know. That's why philosophers and aristocrats living in democracies make good allies. They're fighting similar fights.

Director: Well said. And I think it's probably true. What do you think philosophers are fighting for?

Lawyer: Their freedom.

Director: Freedom from what?

Lawyer: The constraints of any regime. And now you're quiet again.

Director: I'm thinking. I think you're right. There are constraints that come with any regime. Philosophers don't like those constraints. But does anyone really like constraint?

Lawyer: Aristocrats do. Think of it as the resistance that makes us grow tall and straight.

Director: That's really very interesting. I never thought of it that way. So are you saying philosophers don't grow tall and straight? Maybe tall but not straight? Or maybe straight but not tall?

Lawyer: Ha, ha. Don't take offense. It's just a metaphor, my friend.

Director: But metaphors can cut to the quick. I wouldn't dare use a metaphor against you.

Lawyer: You're too sensitive for your own good. And here I thought philosophers had to be tough.

Director: Some philosophers are very sensitive. Rousseau comes to mind. Some philosophers are very tough. Schopenhauer comes to mind. But as soon as I say that I think I might be mistaken. Things along these lines are very hard to know.

Lawyer: Who else is sensitive and who tough? I'm interested to hear.

Director: Sure, you aristocrats love the juicy gossip. Kierkegaard, I'd say, is very sensitive. Xenophon is very tough. But, again, I have my doubts about the categorization.

Lawyer: Let me guess. You think philosophers must be peculiar blend of sensitive and tough.

Director: Yes, of course. Any human being needs this blend—you included. Look at you. You're a lion in court.

Lawyer: And?

Director: And you're a regular pussycat with your friends.

Lawyer: That's how you view me? As a pussycat?

Director: Well, certainly a cat. Cats can be so gentle and sweet—and they can claw your eyes out when things turn.

Lawyer: Do you really think I'd claw your eyes out?

Director: If my eyes needed clawing, I think you'd be the one. But seriously, my point is that you can be both very gentle and a fierce fighter when needed.

Lawyer: Like a dog? I'm gentle with the ones I love and fierce with the enemy?

Director: Yes, but dogs assume the enemy is the unknown.

Lawyer: And philosophers don't.

Director: No, philosophers are very much like dogs. They attack the unknown—and hope to make it... known.

Lawyer: What kind of attack is this?

Director: A barrage of words. Words, words, and more words—until the city walls are breached.

Lawyer: And then you rush in.

Director: No, actually. We sit there a long while and wonder if the inhabitants of the pierced city will venture forth.

Lawyer: And if they don't?

Director: We dip a toe in the water and see.

50

Lawyer: You don't mind mixing your metaphors.

Director: Not in the least. Sorry if you find it annoying.

Lawyer: I find it more interesting than annoying. The water makes me think of a moat around a castle.

Director: Ah, I had forgotten. Aristocrats of old loved their castles. What's the new castle?

Lawyer: Oh, I don't know. Gated communities?

Director: Yes, it would probably have to be something like that. Even in a digital age physical security takes priority.

Lawyer: Certainly. And the infrastructure of the digital is emphatically physical. We'll have to ensure control of that.

Director: Good Committee work, no doubt. Tell me. Who is more likely to think the virtual frees us from the physical—a democrat or an aristocrat?

Lawyer: The democrat. Democrats are dreamers; aristocrats are very much grounded in the real.

Director: Does that mean they lack imagination?

Lawyer: I.... No.

Director: You started to say something?

Lawyer: I think democrats place more value on imagination than aristocrats do. Yes, aristocrats want creative thinking to help them in rule. But they don't long for works of imagination to take them away. They like where they are.

Director: I see. So democrats have more incentive to develop their imagination.

Lawyer: I don't like to concede the ground, but I think it's true.

Director: When it comes to works of art, aristocrats will tend toward realism?

Lawyer: I don't know if I'd call it realism, but I'd say they would prefer Racine to Rousseau.

Director: They like something more severe.

Lawyer: Formal, I'd call it.

Director: Less philosophical, I'd call it. And they prefer Xenophon to Plato?

Lawyer: Xenophon, after all, wrote a treatise on the hunt. How could aristocrats not like that? But they never forget that Plato was born of the highest nobility. And he envisioned a society in which the philosophers—read nobles—rule.

Director: That was ironic. He turned anti-philosophers into philosophers. Quite a feat. Sometimes I wonder how you could be an aristocrat.

Lawyer: Me? What do you mean?

Director: You express interest in philosophy. You even talk about bringing philosophers to your regime.

Lawyer: Philosophy is the love of wisdom. That's what the name literally means. I love wisdom. And I believe the oldest wisdom is best.

Director: Why do you believe that?

Lawyer: Because it's passed the test of time.

Director: But you know how it goes. A work is in favor for a couple of centuries, then it is obscured; later it makes a comeback, only to fall again from grace.

Lawyer: But all that back and forth is precisely the test of time. The bad works never enter the cycle. They have their day then fall away and die. Give me something that stirs up controversy—it's a sign of life.

Director: I didn't know aristocrats go looking for controversy.

Lawyer: A lot of them don't. But it's something I relish.

Director: That's the real reason you want a resident philosopher. You want him to stir things up.

Lawyer: A flaw of aristocracy is stasis. I want a counter to that.

Director: But I thought aristocrats are always striving.

Lawyer: Sometimes it's good not to strive. Sometimes it's good to sit back and learn.

Director: Are you saying there is a sort of inertia to constant motion?

Lawyer: Yes. And I'm saying constant motion is often used to suppress the urge to think.

51

Director: You want your aristocrats to think—in order to better rule?

Lawyer: Yes, of course that. But also to better live. As you've pointed out, there is more to life than rule.

Director: So even if philosophy merely shows people how to enjoy themselves best, it's worth it?

Lawyer: I really believe it is. Enjoying yourself is no small thing.

Director: Do you believe you should enjoy rule? Or do you think it's only a matter of satisfaction?

Lawyer: This is something I could learn from philosophy—the difference between satisfaction and enjoyment. Maybe they're the same thing. I don't know—but I'm willing to learn.

Director: So am I. I'd be happy to discuss this with your peers.

Lawyer: You'd be happy to discuss this with anyone.

Director: With anyone who cared. Will your peers care?

Lawyer: They're concerned with excellence. Part of that involves clearness, cleanliness of mind. Philosophy can help them here.

Director: Well, a clean mind is good for rule and other things, too. I'd be happy to talk to them. But there's one condition. If I get the sense like they're not truly engaged, I stop. Oh, and there's a second condition. I'll only talk with very small groups.

Lawyer: What happens if you're speaking with a group of four, and one person isn't engaged?

Director: I'd stop talking, or I'd ask them to leave. The latter might create hard feelings, you know.

Lawyer: Among the unengaged? Yes, I think that's true. You might tweak their pride. But it's a shame to let one person ruin it for the rest. Why not just let them stay?

Director: They'd be a distraction for the others—and for me.

Lawyer: Maybe the others have to handle the situation, not you. They are the person's peers, after all.

Director: Yes, and I'd have no rank or authority. But things might get ugly and then no one would be in the frame of mind required to make things clear.

Lawyer: You have to be at peace to make things clear, don't you?

Director: You have to be focused. There might be war in your soul, but you focus for the time being because you want to know.

Lawyer: Is that what you are? Someone who wants to know?

Director: Not primarily, no.

Lawyer: Then what are you? I thought all philosophers want to know.

Director: Knowledge is a tool used in living a good life. So we want to know, of course. But that's not the end in itself.

Lawyer: So you're with the ancient Greek philosophers here. The good life is the highest end. And I'm with you. And I believe aristocracy is the means to living this best life.

Director: But the ancients believed the life dedicated to philosophy was best. So is it aristocracy for the sake of philosophy?

Lawyer: Maybe... for some.

Director: Some like you?

Lawyer: Look, you can't philosophize all the time, right? I mean, you get tired. What if I exercise in the morning, rule during the day, and philosophize with others at night. That sounds like the perfect life to me.

Director: Somehow that seems appropriate—you have to philosophize under cover of darkness in an aristocratic regime.

Lawyer: Would you do it?

Director: Maybe I could be a visitor now and then. I'd come, stay for a couple of weeks, and then move on.

Lawyer: Why move on? Why not stay for good?

Director: Two reasons. One, I wouldn't be a peer; two, we all need time to digest. Philosophy involves taking in a lot of things. If you don't break it down, you'll grow upset.

Lawyer: What, like an upset stomach?

Director: Yes, exactly that—the stomach in your mind.

52

Lawyer: But there's also a very real connection between mental disturbance and actual stomach problems.

Director: No doubt there is. Mental disturbance leads to all kinds of problems.

Lawyer: So you're saying we need to stir then let things settle down.

Director: Not quite. We need to keep stirring—but each has to learn to do it on their own.

Lawyer: And once we get used to the stirring and do it all the time?

Director: I'd say you would have become a philosopher. But here's the thing. When you converse with others you can't let them shut you down. You stir, and when you talk, you can't help but start to stir them.

Lawyer: That sounds like trouble. Not everyone wants to be stirred. Some react violently to attempts.

Director: Yes, I'm aware of the problem. Still, you have to ask yourself if you want to have peers who can't or won't be stirred.

Lawyer: That sounds like worse trouble.

Director: Are you sure? Many perfectly satisfied aristocrats through the ages have never been stirred out of their belief in themselves.

Lawyer: Is that what we're talking about? Stirring up our belief in ourselves?

Director: In some ways, all knowledge is connected to our belief in ourselves. The more we know, the greater the challenge.

Lawyer: I don't see how that is.

Director: Belief in self involves certain ways of existing with our surroundings. Learning more about the surroundings, we learn more about ourselves. Does that make sense?

Lawyer: Yes, that's very basic and true.

Director: Well, there's more to it than that, but I think that's a good place to start.

Lawyer: You mean it also holds for our relationships with people? Learn more about them and learn more about yourself?

Director: Yes, you get the idea. This learning needs to be broken down and absorbed. That takes time. A couple of weeks is the maximum I could stay. I'd need to retreat then and digest what I've learned.

Lawyer: Oh, I didn't think you were the one who needed a break! I thought you were saying my peers and I were the ones.

Director: I wouldn't be teaching in these sessions. I'd be philosophizing with you. We would be equals here.

Lawyer: Philosophical peers.

Director: Yes. Do you think your aristocratic peers could bring themselves to respect me as a peer?

Lawyer: Not all of them, no. But some of them could.

Director: Would you have me visit to philosophize with these some—under cover of darkness?

Lawyer: I'm afraid that might be necessary. I'm not willing to sacrifice philosophy because some of my peers can't be bothered to stir.

Director: Those who don't like to stir themselves don't like others to stir them, either. It's a sort of natural law. If a majority of your peers like to stir, things will be fine. But if it's just a small minority....

Lawyer: The cover of darkness it is. But word will get out. How could it not? And when it does we'll seem guilty for trying to hide.

Director: Then you'll have to do two things. One, you must be open with others about the discussions; two, you have to ensure that the people who attend are the most distinguished and of the highest rank.

Lawyer: I understand. But being open about the discussions is different than being open about exactly what was said.

Director: That will tantalize others.

Lawyer: That and the fact that those of the highest rank attend.

Director: Of course. Tantalizing can be a step toward stirring. Philosophy can be a perk of the highest ranks in your state.

Lawyer: Doesn't that put a lot of pressure on you?

Director: I'm used to a considerable amount of pressure. But I don't think the pressure will be so bad. We'll just talk like you and I are talking today.

53

Lawyer: I'm not sure that's a good idea. We've said a fair amount that cuts against aristocracy.

Director: We have to hear the bad to do the good. Your peers will undoubtedly know some of aristocracy's flaws. Discussion is the first step toward overcoming.

Lawyer: Maybe it's how it is with children and adults. Children you give the prettier story; adults must deal with the ugly facts.

Director: Sometimes I wonder if that's a mistake. Youths can handle quite a bit. Sometimes they even see things more clearly than adults.

Lawyer: Sometimes, sure. But aristocracies can be volatile places. Our conversations must be held in confidence.

Director: Okay. But why are aristocracies so volatile? Jealousies as we said?

Lawyer: No doubt that. But also because there's constant pressure from the plebs.

Director: Pressure to keep them down. I can see how that might tell with time.

Lawyer: There's nothing quite like the feeling of going to bed knowing there's a large number of people who would like nothing better than to kill you in your sleep. It changes you over time.

Director: Do they really resent you that much?

Lawyer: Maybe not at first. But over time, once the aristocracy is fully established? They will hate us for what we are.

Director: Parasites.

Lawyer: No! Look at you smile!

Director: I couldn't resist. You are the excellent, and the less than excellent will hate you for this. Is that how it goes?

Lawyer: That's how it goes.

Director: Where does justice fit in all of this?

Lawyer: Well, we'll have control of the courts. And there will be no laws for us.

Director: Just to be sure—the plebs will have plenty of laws.

Lawyer: Oh yes, they certainly will.

Director: Laws will help keep them in place. And no one of the plebs will be above the law.

Lawyer: Right. They must fear the law, and obey it in their hearts.

Director: It's not enough to obey the law in fact?

Lawyer: No, the plebs must be docile. You can obey the laws in fact and be a rebel in your heart.

Director: Rebels are so interesting. To a ruler a rebel is a threat. To many outside of rule a rebel is admired. You see this often in democratic popular culture.

Lawyer: That's because democrats are suspicious of rule.

Director: Except when they're corrupt?

Lawyer: Corruption for them means to place their hopes in being saved.

Director: I don't understand. They expect the ruler to save them?

Lawyer: An incorrupt democracy saves itself. A corrupt democracy wants someone else to do this for them.

Director: It's as simple as that? Save or be saved?

Lawyer: It is. And an aristocracy worth its salt never asks for help. It's much too proud.

Director: So if we see an aristocracy asking for help, we know things are in a very bad way.

54

Lawyer: Tell me something, Director. Do philosophers ever ask for help?

Director: All the time. When we're stuck in our thought we go begging high and low for anything that can lend a hand.

Lawyer: A hand in thought? That doesn't sound right. I thought we think alone.

Director: Yes, we digest alone. But sometimes the meal needs more meat, starch, or spice. I'm not shy about asking my friends for any of them.

Lawyer: But that's the thing. You ask your friends. You don't go around begging your enemies.

Director: No, you're right to chastise me here. I don't beg my enemies. I do, however, make use of whatever I can steal from them.

Lawyer: That's interesting. Spartan aristocratic youth were taught at a young age to steal without being caught.

Director: Why do you think that was?

Lawyer: I don't know. I've often wondered what the reason was. I suppose it has to do with the virtues of war. There's nothing wrong in stealing from enemies.

Director: Because all is fair in love and war? But this makes me think of your political marriages. Will illicit affairs flourish when one can't wed for love?

Lawyer: Remember what I said about jealousies? Here is a cause.

Director: But why be jealous if you don't love your spouse?

Lawyer: People are funny in their senses of honor.

Director: So it's fine as long as you don't get caught?

Lawyer: I think that's the lesson the Spartans drew.

Director: Alcibiades the Athenian got a child off the Spartan queen, they say. Was he more practiced in the arts of the Spartans than they were themselves?

Lawyer: Good old Alcibiades the hero, then traitor, then hero. He had many skills. But mention of the queen reminds me that the Spartan regime wasn't all aristocrats. It was mixed.

Director: The English regime was mixed. The Venetian regime was mixed. The French regime was mixed. The other Italian regimes were... well, a little bit too crazy to say what they were.

Lawyer: You think our regime should be mixed?

Director: It might just happen on its own.

Lawyer: Who would be our king?

Director: Maybe you would be the king.

Lawyer: How would that happen?

Director: There might be a crisis, say a crisis with the plebs. Your regime might require a sort of Roman dictator to lead them into the clear. This might require you to take on certain powers, powers not easily set down.

Lawyer: Yes, I see what you mean. Regimes are living things; they always shift and often grow.

Director: That's why the founders of our democracy worked in a degree of flexibility to the regime.

Lawyer: People who know speak of a flexible republic, not a democracy. The republic fails if it becomes completely democratic.

Director: A direct democracy.

Lawyer: Yes, that horror of horrors. That's what happened to Athens. Then it collapsed.

Director: Some say that's why it lost the war with Sparta.

Lawyer: It lost because it recalled Alcibiades from leading the expedition against Sicily, to bring him up on capital charges.

Director: Yes, he outraged the gods by desecrating their statues, they say. There's no answer to that but death. And so he turned traitor and fled to Sparta.

Lawyer: I was always impressed they took him in.

Director: How could they not? He was a fascinating man.

Lawyer: Didn't he later flee to Persia?

Director: He did. He went from democracy, to aristocracy, to kingship.

Lawyer: And then he retired into lawless lands, where he was found by assassins and killed.

Director: That's often what happens when you cross too many lines.

Lawyer: That's a lesson to us—not to take in a fascinating enemy.

Director: What would you do with him?

Lawyer: Cut him down to size.

55

Director: The Spartans used to murder their fascinating plebs. Is that what you suggest?

Lawyer: No, these are different times. We would simply make it hard for him to find a job.

Director: Economic death. A slower sort of torture. What makes someone fascinating?

Lawyer: What made Alcibiades fascinating? He was noble, handsome, rich, clever, treacherous.

Director: One of your plebs could only be handsome, rich, and clever. I don't think you'd allow any treachery.

Lawyer: No, we wouldn't—not even among our own. But you mention that he could be rich. I don't feel like we've tied this down. We started by saying we'd do away with the super rich, but we said we'd leave the plebs' economy more or less intact—but have we said how rich we'd let someone become?

Director: Who cares what we said? What do we say now?

Lawyer: I don't think anyone should be half as rich as the poorest of the aristocrats. I don't want them to get any funny ideas.

Director: That sounds fine to me. And who knows? Maybe their economy will work better without the clotting effect of the rich.

Lawyer: What clots an aristocracy?

Director: Those who won't relinquish high honors. For instance, let's say you have an appointed commander in chief. The position lasts for a year. At the end of the year he doesn't want to step down. This might happen, no?

Lawyer: Of course. That's why there has to be honor in stepping down.

Director: Honor and some sort of money reward. Honor isn't always enough.

Lawyer: A rich pension, sure. That makes sense.

Director: And certain other privileges.

Lawyer: Like what?

Director: Oh, I don't know. He gets to sit in a special seat at sporting events. Things like that.

Lawyer: Yes, I see what you mean. I, for one, would look forward to money and special privilege. I know that about myself.

Director: Which would be more important to you? The money or the privilege?

Lawyer: The privilege.

Director: Why?

Lawyer: I'm an aristocrat at heart. Honors always mean more than money to me.

Director: Provided you have your certain base income.

Lawyer: That goes without saying. But what about a philosopher? Honors, too?

Director: No, nor money. Opportunity is what I want. Opportunity to talk.

Lawyer: With whom?

Director: The queen of Sparta.

Lawyer: That's all you want? To talk?

Director: The right conversation with the right person at the right time can move the world.

Lawyer: Ah, you want to rule the world. I knew you were more ambitious than I am!

Director: No, I'm not looking to rule. I'm looking to tilt the world a degree.

Lawyer: Why?

Director: I want to free certain people up.

56

Lawyer: I don't know if you've freed me up, but you're certainly making me think.

Director: And you will tilt the world.

Lawyer: You don't do it yourself?

Director: We each have to put in our own effort here. I give a nudge. You give a nudge. Our friends give a nudge. Soon the world has moved, if only a bit. But that bit can be enough—to free certain others up.

Lawyer: Free them to rule?

Director: Some of them, yes.

Lawyer: And that's justice? That's what they deserve?

Director: If you were freed to rule, would justice be done?

Lawyer: Yes.

Director: Why?

Lawyer: I will do my best without ulterior motives. I have shown I know human nature in my dealings in the courts. I have a tremendous work ethic. My thoughts are tempered by philosophy. I believe in myself, but not as an absolute. I am fair and not out for any sort of revenge. Finally, rule would satisfy my basic need. We all need that.

Director: And you don't think rule is for us all?

Lawyer: No, I honestly don't. Look at you. Do you have a basic need to rule?

Director: I don't. But maybe philosophers are the exception.

Lawyer: No, philosophers are not alone in this. Plenty of people don't want to rule.

Director: But does that mean they need to be ruled?

Lawyer: Yes. And yes, philosophers are exceptions to the law of rule or be ruled.

Director: Why are philosophers exceptional?

Lawyer: They rule themselves and themselves alone

Director: Hmm. That's nice to think, but I'm not sure that's how it goes. Maybe philosophers rule nothing at all, not even themselves.

Lawyer: Philosophers allow themselves to be ruled?

Director: No, not that—not for what counts.

Lawyer: What do you mean?

Director: I mean, if the rulers say you must wear this costume in your daily life, I say fine. I will wear the costume. If the rulers say you must not eat this and only eat that, I will probably say fine. I will obey the dietary laws. But if the rulers ask me to bring the sacrifice of the mind? I will not. And rulers more often demand the sacrifice of the mind than anything else.

Lawyer: You would rebel.

Director: I would have no choice.

Lawyer: Would you subvert the regime?

Director: Apparently the rulers believe that thinking subverts. So, on those terms, I would subvert the regime.

Lawyer: How do rulers demand the sacrifice of the intellect?

Director: It's very simple. Take one part threat of force, and one part don't-think-about-that; stir vigorously; and there you have it.

Lawyer: Aristocrats want their plebs to sacrifice the intellect, don't they?

Director: Yes, they do. They insist. Sparta murdered the intellect as much as it murdered the body—more so even, in absolute terms.

Lawyer: I don't like this business of the sacrifice of the intellect.

Director: Then you're angling for the wrong regime. But it's worse than you think.

Lawyer: How so?

Director: Aristocrats want to bring each other the sacrifice of mind.

57

Lawyer: Why would they want that?

Director: What belief do they need?

Lawyer: Belief in themselves and their regime.

Director: If I stroll in there questioning them and their regime, how do you think they'll react?

Lawyer: Yes, yes. But democrats would do the exact same thing!

Director: True. But do you know who wouldn't?

Lawyer: An open minded king.

Director: Yes, and then everyone would have to go along.

Lawyer: So philosophers hope for kings to come to power?

Director: No, because the odds of a king being open minded like this are very small. They, too, need to believe in themselves and their regime.

Lawyer: Who doesn't need to believe in themselves and their regime? A tyrant? Tyrants are too busy worrying about other things to bother much with belief. Maybe you should turn to them.

Director: Plato did that, you know. He went to Syracuse to meet Dionysius the tyrant. It didn't turn out well.

Lawyer: How could it? Philosophers can be such fools. That's one of the reasons I'm merely an aristocrat sympathetic to philosophy, and not a philosopher myself. It's almost as if some of them had their prudence gene removed at birth.

Director: That's a conscious choice.

Lawyer: What do you mean?

Director: Philosophers sometimes have to sacrifice prudence for something more important.

Lawyer: Like what?

Director: Dialogue. A conversation is only as good as what each party offers. It might be prudent to keep your mouth shut. But sometimes opening up is the only way to proceed. You have to give something to get something. And that involves risk.

Lawyer: It's no doubt risky to open your heart and mind to another. I take the point, Director. Is that why philosophers often find themselves in impossible situations?

Director: It's a big part of it, yes. Say too much and then you can't go back. This lends a certain drive to a philosopher's life.

Lawyer: What do you hope to get out of these conversations?

Director: Understanding.

Lawyer: Your own or theirs?

Director: Both—and something more. A check on belief.

Lawyer: What does that mean?

Director: We all—all of us—are in danger of going wild in our beliefs. We need to examine them and pull out the weeds.

Lawyer: So you're worried that in questioning someone's beliefs you'll give offense.

Director: Yes.

Lawyer: That's understandable. Maybe that's why you'd only stay a couple of weeks in our aristocracy. You're afraid.

Director: Philosophers are not immune to fear. It takes time for certain lines of questioning to sink in and take effect. Sometimes people appreciate them; sometimes they come to resent. Imagine lowly me dealing with mighty aristocrats. Do you blame me for wanting to limit my exposure, for wanting to see how things develop before I go forward?

Lawyer: No, I don't blame you. You truly would be stepping into the lion's den—especially if you came from our plebs. If you came from another country, it would be easier to suffer your questions.

Director: Suffer them? That's an apt expression.

Lawyer: Oh, you know what I mean.

Director: Yes, I do.

58

Lawyer: It's all about the odds, you know.

Director: In life it's often that way. But what do you mean?

Lawyer: We select the few, establish them in their roles, and hope most of them turn out to be good. It's the same with their descendants—we can only hope they'll turn out to be good. But I believe the odds are that they will. Do you know what I mean?

Director: Very few things are certain, yes. That's why it's often best to roll with things and let circumstances determine fate.

Lawyer: Fatalism? But many of us rise above our circumstances.

Director: Here is a heresy for the democrats. What happens when these people rise above? They spend the rest of their lives in a terrible struggle.

Lawyer: Are you suggesting it might be better not to rise above? To be crushed?

Director: Not to be crushed, no; but not to strive to rise above. Step out of the way, but keep to your level.

Lawyer: So a pleb shouldn't long to be an aristocrat?

Director: And an aristocrat shouldn't want to be king.

Lawyer: But what about rising above through education?

Director: Ambitious education? What do you really learn other than what will get you above or ahead? Where's the excellence in that?

Lawyer: Do you believe in learning for its own sake?

Director: Do you?

Lawyer: I do. Knowledge is like gold. It's always good to have.

Director: And if you find a good way to spend it?

Lawyer: You can always get more.

Director: While I'm inclined to agree, I think there's an important distinction to make. There is knowledge, and then there are facts. We can always get more facts; some are harder to obtain than others, true; but, in theory, we can always get more.

Lawyer: Then what is knowledge? The digestion of facts?

Director: Precisely. And maybe I should emphasize something a little bit more. Some facts are very, very hard to obtain. Some people would die to obtain them. As if that weren't enough, these facts can be very, very hard to digest.

Lawyer: Can you take the facts on trust from another?

Director: What? Yes, I suppose. But it's not the same.

Lawyer: No, I didn't think it was. I'll be honest. I'm not really motivated to go after such facts. Some brave reporter might be. Good for him. And good for me to watch him from the comfort of home.

Director: Do you think it's hard to digest those reported facts?

Lawyer: Sure. But you can take them or leave them. If you've gained them first hand, that's not really an option.

Director: Certain facts haunt?

Lawyer: The certainly do. Try as you might to brush them aside, they tug at you in your dreams.

Director: If you're lucky enough to sleep.

Lawyer: True.

Director: Will the few brush aside the facts concerning the many?

Lawyer: That's a big fear of mine, you know. They might be more worthy than we think.

Director: Worthy of what?

Lawyer: Ha! That's a very good question.

Director: Worthy of rule?

Lawyer: No, I'm not concerned with that. I'm confident the few are better at rule.

Director: Worthy of admiration?

Lawyer: That's the thing. I admire their pluck.

Director: But?

Lawyer: This isn't the generation that won the second world war.

59

Director: You think things are on the decline.

Lawyer: I know they are. Everyone is so entitled today.

Director: Everyone?

Lawyer: No, but that's the center of gravity here, despite some great exceptions.

Director: Do you think those exceptions will make for good aristocrats? Or no, what am I saying? Aristocrats are the most entitled people on Earth!

Lawyer: You're always so funny. Some of these people would make very good aristocrats.

Director: And all you have to do is tap them on arm and say, 'You're in.'

Lawyer: This is the heart of the problem. The selection. I won't have that power. I don't know who will have that power, or how this will work. It's all just a dream until we can work this out.

Director: You're going to have to choose from people already in power, possibly with a few exceptions here and there that everyone can agree on.

Lawyer: When you say 'in power', you don't mean in democratically elected positions, do you?

Director: No, you're going to need people who have money. Lots of money.

Lawyer: The super rich? How many of them do you think there are?

Director: I don't know. What's that list they publish? I think I saw there were around 2,000 billionaires in the world. Maybe that's the global aristocracy.

Lawyer: That's an oligarchy, not an aristocracy.

Director: You aristocrats are so touchy on that. Oligarchy is the rule of the few, regardless of their qualities; aristocracy is the rule of the excellent, the best. But billionaires are excellent at handling money. Aren't they?

Lawyer: Call it what it is—a plutocracy; rule by wealth.

Director: And you really don't want that.

Lawyer: I really don't. I really want wealth, but not excessive wealth. Wealth enough to live free. Democrats can understand that desire. Some of them might have sympathy with us.

Director: Don't count on too much of that. So you merely rich lawyers are going to have to team up. What is that called?

Lawyer: What is what called?

Director: Rule by well to do lawyers. Hmm. I can't seem to think of a name. Maybe this is something new. You may have stumbled on to something new!

Lawyer: What about the entrepreneurs, the bankers, and so on?

Director: Yes, I suppose they deserve a place. But they must have excellence and not just wealth. How can we tell?

Lawyer: We can tell by how they treat their people.

Director: Are you talking about servant leaders again? Do aristocrats rule for the sake of the plebs?

Lawyer: No. And this is where people's heart must grow hard. Aristocrats rule for the sake of human excellence.

Director: So you're looking for leaders who exploit the ones they rule.

Lawyer: I... don't know. Are you talking about exploiting for the sake of excellence?

Director: I am. And I don't mean you need to be cruel all the time. I just mean you're willing for them to work to support yourselves.

Lawyer: I am willing for them to work for that. Of course, not everything they earn goes to us. They'll live a good life—probably better than before.

Director: Lawyer, if that's what you need to ease your conscience, I am all in favor of it. Aristocracy is good for many and few alike. Go with it. You've been awfully hard on yourself.

Lawyer: I honestly think it's true! We'll be better at managing things than their elected leaders ever could be on their own. We'll guide them into decisions that make sense. After all, we'll have a financial interest in their success! Think of us as shareholders of the corporate regime. We want everyone to prosper.

60

Director: One word and the floodgates open.

Lawyer: Do you think it's untrue?

Director: That you want your plebs to do well? No, I don't. As you say, you'll have an interest here. You just don't want them to do... too well.

Lawyer: To do too well is to be unwell.

Director: The billionaires do too well. Do you agree?

Lawyer: For most of them? Yes.

Director: What's this new qualification?

Lawyer: There are exceptions here like everywhere else.

Director: So you'd take a billionaire into you're few.

Lawyer: As long as he shed some wealth, yes.

Director: How many billionaires are there in the United States?

Lawyer: Around 600.

Director: That's 12 for every state.

Lawyer: Well, they concentrate in certain states.

Director: Even so, isn't that number good for an aristocracy? Six hundred over 300,000,000 total population? What's the percentage there?

Lawyer: The results on my calculator come out in notation. 2e-6.

Director: Let's see. That's 0.000002. Am I right?

Lawyer: I don't know. But the percentage is certainly small.

Director: I don't know either. But I agree—the percentage is certainly small. How many rich lawyers are there in the United States?

Lawyer: I don't think that's the question to ask. I think we have to ask how many partners are there in top tier firms.

Director: These would be aristocrats?

Lawyer: They're wealthy; cultured, for the most part; and experienced in rule.

Director: You mean they rule their associates, paralegals, and secretaries? And where do they get their culture? A once a season trip to the symphony?

Lawyer: What's wrong with the symphony? They like that, and the ballet, and Shakespeare, and reading all the great books.

Director: And all of this ensures they're the best. Tell me, and tell me true. Do they like these things for their own sake? Or do they like them because they confer cultural distinction?

Lawyer: Of course some people are snobs. But I, for one, honesty love Shakespeare.

Director: Many people do, even among the plebs. In fact, many of the plebs love all of these cultural things. What do you say to that?

Lawyer: More power to them.

Director: Would you like to have a culture peculiar to the few?

Lawyer: I would.

Director: When was the last time aristocrats had world class culture at their sole disposal?

Lawyer: Well, I can't help but think of an American. John Singer Sargent.

Director: You're including as aristocrats the wealthy democrats he portrayed?

Lawyer: They would have been aristocrats if given the chance.

Director: Maybe they were aristocrats.

Lawyer: Democrats only in name?

Director: Could you be content with that?

Lawyer: When was the 17th Amendment ratified?

Director: Excuse me?

Lawyer: Do you know when?

Director: 1913.

Lawyer: They were aristocrats to that point.

Director: You're being rather dramatic.

Lawyer: Direct election of senators changed everything. Before the amendment the people didn't have a real say. This amendment changed their expectations.

Director: The senators were no longer of the ruling class?

Lawyer: They were, but direct election changed what they could do or say.

Director: Would you overturn the amendment?

Lawyer: No. I would just weaken what these weak senators can do.

61

Director: If you think an American senator is weak, what do you think makes one strong?

Lawyer: Look to my peers and you'll see.

Director: Do you believe the people make this country strong?

Lawyer: Some of the people, sure. And the country would be stronger still with a healthy few in the lead.

Director: But if you're leading the people, the people must be strong—or you'll be weak. No? I mean, your income depends on their economic strength.

Lawyer: True. A bold aristocracy allows for a healthy plebs. It's symbiosis.

Director: The few depend on the plebs. You admit as much?

Lawyer: I do. It's the truth.

Director: You're more true than many an aristocrat. They would never avow their dependence on the plebs.

Lawyer: Has there ever been an aristocracy that followed on a democracy?

Director: An interesting question. We'll have to turn to the historians. You aristocrats love history, don't you? Why?

Lawyer: Aristocracies are always under threat, and often short lived. They turn to the history of their own for moral support.

Director: Short lived? Venice lasted a thousand years.

Lawyer: Venice was a republic.

Director: So is America.

Lawyer: So I have another eight hundred years to wait?

Director: Maybe. But there's something I've noticed about aristocrats. Regimes change, but the nobility still keeps track of births and descent.

Lawyer: They're waiting for the next chance.

Director: Yes. But nothing like that is happening in America. There are no nobles to keep track of, births and descent. The closest thing we have is the Daughters of the American Revolution—and that was a revolution against aristocracy.

Lawyer: Technically it was a revolution against the king.

Director: Who led the aristocracy. Britain was a mixed regime.

Lawyer: True. Do you think that made it strong?

Director: Yes. It's what makes America strong. But you, you want to un-mix the regime. You want a pure aristocracy.

Lawyer: As pure as I can get.

Director: Well, you're going to have it hard. You have no ancient titles; you have no god given claim to rule. You only have your virtue, your excellence.

Lawyer: That should be enough.

Director: And if your offspring show no virtue? Do they still get to rule?

Lawyer: Nothing is perfect. Didn't we talk about this? What do you want us to do, have life peerages? The problem with that is who creates them. We don't even have a House of Lords to work with. We're in a desert.

Director: Ah, poor thirsty soul. Perhaps the water of politics will refresh you. You know how deeply political a move your aristocracy is. All the ugliness of politics will come to the fore when it's time to name the nobility.

Lawyer: I expect as much. That's why it's important to have a core of trusted friends before this all starts.

Director: Friends to ensure each other gets in.

Lawyer: And gets in early, to influence the rest. That's the key to everything here.

Director: I agree. But, my friend, this is starting to sound like a conspiracy again.

Lawyer: When things look bad you have to plan.

Director: What's the difference between planning and conspiring?

Lawyer: I don't know. Do you?

Director: I don't. So maybe it's best not to plan, Lawyer.

Lawyer: We can't just sit back and do nothing if things start to go to hell, Director.

Director: No, that's true. But I feel like we've said enough—and maybe more than enough. So take things as they come. And whatever you do, don't conspire.

Lawyer: What about you? What will you do?

Director: I will do what I always do. Talk.

Lawyer: They put Socrates to death for talk.

Director: Yes, a certain kind of talk. I'll try not to have that happen to me. But in the meantime, let's go and find some food!

* * *

PART TWO

SETTING: A CAMBRIDGE RESTAURANT, FRIDAY EVENING

62

Lawyer: This is my favorite place.

Director: Elegant dining, yes. But won't they be itching to have us eat then hurry us out? There's a significant wait for a table.

Lawyer: No, for two reasons. One, that's not a classy thing to do. Two, I know the owner and he always insists I stay as long as I like.

Director: You've done some legal work for him?

Lawyer: How did you guess?

Director: And you did it for free.

Lawyer: Yes. It was nothing.

Director: So you won yourself an elegant perch. Very nice.

Lawyer: Yes. But what were you saying before the waiter came by?

Director: When we were speaking of your aristocracy, we spoke of an income the few would receive from taxes on the plebs. But we didn't speak of any property they'd hold.

Lawyer: Are you talking about land? The landed aristocracy? That's from when the income from land was great.

Director: What if you owned the land in downtown Boston? What if you leased the land to business people? Wouldn't that income be great?

Lawyer: Sure. But how do we get cities to grant us land that someone already owns? The tax we discussed is a less painful thing. Here we're talking about confiscation.

Director: But it would work so much nicer for you. You could be Marquess of Boston. Someone else could be Duke of New York. And so on.

Lawyer: Ha, ha. Maybe in another thousand years, Director.

Director: But seriously, what property will you have?

Lawyer: Well, we'll own our homes, that we'll purchase like anyone else. We'll have our cars. Some will have boats, a second home, and so on.

Director: What about your bank accounts? Your securities? The money in your pocket?

Lawyer: What about them?

Director: That's property, too.

Lawyer: Sure. Knowing that, maybe you should have been a lawyer.

Director: Why have property?

Lawyer: What do you mean?

Director: Why have things that belong to you?

Lawyer: So we can have exclusive use of them.

Director: Why do we want that?

Lawyer: You have a condominium, a car, a bank account. Why do you want them?

Director: I guess I'm just going along with everyone else. I don't really want these things as things themselves.

Lawyer: What are you, a communist?

Director: I remember when that was a really dirty word. Now it's lost some of its bite.

Lawyer: That's because communism is no longer an existential threat.

Director: Property won the Cold War.

Lawyer: What property does won the Cold War.

Director: What does property do?

63

Lawyer: It motivates people to achieve.

Director: And to achieve means to earn money.

Lawyer: Yes.

Director: Do you want your aristocrats to be motivated to achieve?

Lawyer: Well....

Director: You want them to have, not earn. What did you call the earning? Grubbing for money? You said, if I recall, you didn't want your descendants ever to have grubbing thoughts at all.

Lawyer: And I don't.

Director: So your answer about property motivating people to achieve doesn't apply to the few.

Lawyer: I guess it doesn't.

Director: What does property do for the few, the aristocrats?

Lawyer: It gives them ground on which to plant their feet, to stand up tall. That ground is everything.

Director: And standing up tall is how they earn their money?

Lawyer: I don't like to say they earn.

Director: Why not?

Lawyer: They need solid peace of mind. The property will always be theirs, no matter what. They can do great things with that under their feet.

Director: So it's property for the sake of greatness.

Lawyer: Human excellence, yes. It's a way of life.

Director: The way you treat each other.

Lawyer: Yes, we treat each other with the highest respect, with knowledge that we're dealing with the few.

Director: The chosen few.

Lawyer: Right.

Director: And the chosen few will have a birthright.

Lawyer: Of course they will.

Director: And that birthright can never be taken away?

Lawyer: Never.

Director: Can one of the few sell their birthright?

Lawyer: Absolutely not.

Director: Why not?

Lawyer: Because then they'll have no means.

Director: But what if they buy land with their birthright?

Lawyer: There are two points here. One, they have their birthright for a reason—they're supposed to model human excellence. How do we know the person who buys the birthright with land has any excellence? Two, speculation often goes bad. We don't want desperate aristocrats on our hands.

Director: If the few can't sell their birthright, what of the plebs?

Lawyer: What birthright have they got?

Director: Their time.

Lawyer: I don't understand.

Director: Time is property.

Lawyer: But people have to work.

Director: Then let's establish a standard work week, with no exceptions made. If it's forty hours, you can't sell your time to work any more than that. Just as you have your income from taxes, the people will have their time.

Lawyer: I suspect you've spent some time in France.

Director: The people need a real stake in the regime. Maybe we should make it twenty hours a week.

Lawyer: Nothing will get done!

Director: You mean there won't be enough tax money to support the few? I'm sure you can work something out. I mean, if everyone earns half of what they make now, won't there be deflation? And if deflation, won't your reduced income from taxes be worth essentially as much as before?

Lawyer: I don't think it's all that neat and clean.

Director: Well, we need to talk to an economist.

64

Lawyer: An economist will tell you that if there is great deflation, people won't be able to pay their debts. If I owe $1,000, and $500 is the new $1,000—I can't pay enough to cover the debt.

Director: Then we reduce the debts accordingly, according to some deflation index we'll create.

Lawyer: Do you have any kind of idea what sort of trouble that will bring?

Director: Is it more trouble than not being able to establish your aristocracy? The newly increased value of the debt to the creditors amounts to an unjust windfall. Can't we argue something like that and have done?

Lawyer: I suppose you have a point. Time as property. Who would have thought?

Director: I can see you've never been on a cheap vacation before.

Lawyer: What do you mean?

Director: One where part of your discounted stay is the requirement to attend a high pressure sales pitch to buy a vacation time share. There, time is property. Someone owns a week here; someone owns a week there.

Lawyer: I would never buy into such a thing.

Director: But many do. They value time.

Lawyer: Oh, we all value time.

Director: Then give the people what they want—time.

Lawyer: Yes, yes. But there are those who really like to work. They don't know what to do with themselves without a full time job.

Director: That sounds like the exception and not the rule. If I didn't have to work full time, I certainly would find plenty of good things to do. I suspect I'm far from alone. Or don't you have faith that people know what to do?

Lawyer: Gardening, time with children and grandchildren, home improvement, reading, sports, hobbies, crafts. I suppose you have a point.

Director: And what about education? Don't people have a desire to improve themselves and their knowledge and understanding?

Lawyer: True.

Director: You don't sound enthused.

Lawyer: The question is what kind of knowledge and understanding will they want?

Director: What do you mean?

Lawyer: They'll want to know that democracy is best. That's what they'll understand.

Director: You're worried they won't see the point of your aristocracy? Well, what is the point?

Lawyer: To be the best.

Director: At what?

Lawyer: Living.

Director: The plebs will seem to live pretty well.

Lawyer: But it has to do with rule. Rule is a part of the very best life. The plebs won't rule, despite their hobbies and such.

Director: Ah, there's that contempt.

Lawyer: But you know I have a point. We're trying to breed the best rulers history has ever known. Will the plebs thrive under proper aristocratic rule? Absolutely! That's the point. Without our control the twenty hour work week, or whatever, never happens. It happens under us.

Director: The better off the plebs the more stable your rule?

Lawyer: No doubt. Any aristocrat from another age, not blinded by arrogance, would heartily agree.

Director: So is it servant leadership?

Lawyer: No, and I despise the concept. The few rule for the sake of the few. They want the many to thrive—for the sake of the few.

65

Director: The problem of rule is perhaps the oldest problem of man.

Lawyer: I agree.

Director: Why do you think it's a problem?

Lawyer: Because everybody wants to rule the world.

Director: They all see themselves as fit?

Lawyer: No doubt.

Director: What do they need to accomplish their desire?

Lawyer: Property, and lots of it.

Director: Property allows us to rule?

Lawyer: Of course it does. Property can be boiled down to money. And money rules.

Director: You're not serious. You believe excellence rules.

Lawyer: True. I'm kidding. The few don't let money rule them or anyone else. That's why they're refreshing to the subjects of a plutocracy.

Director: Is a pleb who doesn't let money rule a natural aristocrat?

Lawyer: There's a chance. If circumstances are right, who knows? They might join the elite.

Director: And be given an aristocrat's income—and protection from the police.

Lawyer: What are you talking about?

Director: Police protect property. Your newly minted aristocrat's income, and what it buys—a home, for instance—will be protected by the police. No?

Lawyer: Of course.

Director: Does this mean there will be laws? We said the few would have no laws.

Lawyer: The laws would concern the many.

Director: The few would never steal.

Lawyer: They'd have no need or desire. That's part of human excellence.

Director: What does it mean to have to protect what you have by force?

Lawyer: It means you have something others want and can't have.

Director: I want a house like yours. I can't have it. Is it possible for me to steal it?

Lawyer: Of course not. But you might, out of jealousy, try to burn it down. That's where the police come in.

Director: So they can arrest me after I do it.

Lawyer: It's the threat of that arrest that deters.

Director: Property requires deterrence.

Lawyer: Welcome to law 101.

Director: Why can't people know you deserve your property and just leave you alone?

Lawyer: Ha! Because opinions on justice vary.

Director: Justice being getting or having what you deserve.

Lawyer: Yes, Director.

Director: The few will agree you all have what you deserve—your life incomes from taxes on the many.

Lawyer: They no doubt will.

Director: What if someone gets funny on this?

Lawyer: One of the few decides he or she or someone else doesn't deserve what they've got? Trouble.

66

Director: And if one of the many decides the few don't deserve what they've got?

Lawyer: That's a funny thing, isn't it? They're unlikely to say so-and-so doesn't deserve what they've got. They'll say none of them deserve what they've got.

Director: To say so-and-so doesn't deserve, etcetera, implies the others do in fact deserve.

Lawyer: Right. That's the point. They can't be fair.

Director: Ah, the poor aristocrats aren't treated fairly. And what about the natural aristocrats among the many?

Lawyer: We promote them as our lieutenants, as we said. And in the rare case, we make them one of us—if circumstances allow.

Director: Yes, you said that gives the plebs some hope that their descendants might one day be of the few. A useful political tool. You know, once there was an idea of property that was a useful tool.

Lawyer: Oh, what idea?

Director: That labor—mental, physical, whatever—gave right. You're not saying that, are you?

Lawyer: No, I'm not. Being is what I'm about. Being the best; being excellent in human virtue.

Director: Being gives title. But being is very hard to establish. As is virtue.

Lawyer: Not so hard, if you know what you're looking for.

Director: What are you looking for?

Lawyer: Primarily? Excellence in rule.

Director: And what is excellence in rule?

Lawyer: Justice. Giving to everyone what they deserve.

Director: That was a skill once reserved to God.

Lawyer: And now it's a skill our aristocrats possess.

Director: My, and we haven't even had much to drink. You'd really make out your aristocrats to be like God?

Lawyer: Maybe like gods, of the Greek variety.

Director: But those gods weren't just. They often acted on whims. Is that what your chosen few would do?

Lawyer: We live thousands of years away from the Greeks. Our aristocrats would never act on whims.

Director: I don't know, Lawyer. What's to stop them?

Lawyer: Unrest in the plebs.

Director: You mean fear would stop them.

Lawyer: I like to call it prudence.

Director: Call it what you like. I'd like to know how you convince the plebs you deserve the money you get.

Lawyer: We keep the peace. Peace is worth a fortune, no?

Director: The peace among ourselves? Or the peace with other states?

Lawyer: Both. A good aristocrat works well without and within.

Director: But when it comes to war?

Lawyer: Aristocrats are experts here. They train for this all their life, from earliest youth on up.

Director: You can train yourself for something all of your life—and not be good. How do we know aristocrats are good at war?

Lawyer: Because sometimes they're at war with the plebs.

67

Director: So you want it both ways. Credit for keeping the peace; credit for waging war.

Lawyer: Everything in its season.

Director: But your property, no matter what, is always in season.

Lawyer: As I've said, a statesman needs that solid ground to stand upon. If you're uncertain of where you stand, you cannot lead. Property is key.

Director: Is that why we used to have property requirements in order to vote?

Lawyer: It is. With property you have skin in the game. You have something to defend. Property is the ballast in the ship. It helps keep it afloat. It keeps it stable.

Director: Stability, yes. Property lends itself to that. And if the regime is stable but bad? Who corrects it then?

Lawyer: Bad regimes don't stay stable long. Who corrects the situation? The good.

Director: The good among the noble?

Lawyer: Who else? The plebs would like to see the regime collapse.

Director: Even when the rule is good?

Lawyer: No, only when it's bad. They go from thinking the regime is good, to thinking it must fall. There's no in-between. There's no patient correction of things.

Director: Why do you think that is?

Lawyer: They have no skin in the game.

Director: What about their time?

Lawyer: A bad regime would take that away—or worse.

Director: What's worse than taking that time away?

Lawyer: Giving them more. 'We only have to work two hours a day! Hurray!' But then? When things fall apart? Who do they blame?

Director: The few who gave them that time.

Lawyer: Correct. This is always the way when you try to appease the plebs.

Director: You need to be firm?

Lawyer: You need to be tough. Caring, but tough.

Director: Caring in a paternal sort of way?

Lawyer: Exactly so, yes.

Director: The people of this country would never go for that.

Lawyer: Give them a bad enough time over a long stretch of years and you might be surprised what they'd go for or not.

Director: What about their property? Could they keep it intact?

Lawyer: There will be no change in their status. Their money is theirs. Their land is theirs. Whatever else they own is theirs. We want nothing of that. They will simply continue to pay their taxes at the rate they're accustomed to, and we'll take care of the rest.

Director: But if there's no change, what's the change that wins them over?

Lawyer: Better government. Better rule. In both domestic and foreign affairs.

Director: And better government and rule because those of the few are better developed?

Lawyer: Yes, that's right. We're better developed because our property allows.

Director: You need security for this development.

Lawyer: Absolutely. That's something the plebs always lack. You need to know this security from birth. It has to be a part of your being, a part of your soul. Then you are fit for greater things. Then you are fit to rule.

Director: Why exactly? What does security from money bring? What does it afford?

Lawyer: Better judgment. You can see things for what they are, rather than through a lens of need for personal gain.

Director: But aren't aristocrats notoriously thirsty for distinction, for fame? Doesn't that color all that they do?

Lawyer: Sure, in the bad cases.

Director: What do we do about the bad cases?

Lawyer: We have to rein them in.

68

Director: How? Do we threaten to take their security away?

Lawyer: If we're going to wound we might as well kill.

Director: We stop their income and freeze their assets.

Lawyer: We must go further. We have to banish them from the realm.

Director: You aristocrats love to say realm instead of country. So we're going to send them away with no means to provide for themselves? How will they live?

Lawyer: They should have thought about that before they went bad.

Director: Maybe you could give them a small stipend?

Lawyer: What, are you feeling sorry for them? We have to crush them so they don't come back and do us harm.

Director: But in some ways a small stipend is more crushing than nothing at all.

Lawyer: How do you figure?

Director: With nothing, pride and indignation are intact. With a pittance, one lowers oneself to accept. The lowered never come back and attack.

Lawyer: Well, you do have a point. But what if they refuse the pittance?

Director: You have an enemy for life. Beware. But refresh my memory. Do all the aristocrats in the realm have the same income?

Lawyer: Yes.

Director: And do they have investment opportunities to increase their wealth?

Lawyer: No, no way.

Director: Why not?

Lawyer: The danger of pride. If one gains so much more than the others, there is an excuse for arrogance.

Director: The possibility of one gone bad.

Lawyer: Exactly. Excessive pride is a failing.

Director: The few need just the right amount of pride.

Lawyer: This is precisely the business of those who rule. Too much or too little spells doom.

Director: And doom is also bad for the plebs.

Lawyer: Certainly. They have an interest here, too.

Director: Is there anything the plebs can do to help?

Lawyer: Just keep on doing their jobs. And let the aristocrats sort it all out.

Director: And if they can't? We'll have a democratic revolution again?

Lawyer: The aristocrats came to power because the plebs couldn't save themselves. How likely is it they'd be able to save things now?

Director: And that's how you earn your wealth, the taxes from them? You save things now.

Lawyer: Exactly so. We earn through proper rule. Democrats know all too well what improper rule is like. Anti-aristocratic sentiments are so many prejudices to be gotten over. When the benefits of our rule are felt, prejudice melts away.

Director: Ah, the aristocrats are the sun that melts the ice. Is it important to you to earn?

Lawyer: It's important to me to deserve. The idea of earning is plebeian in nature.

Director: What's the difference between the two?

Lawyer: When you earn, you don't have. I earn a salary. I work, and then they pay me. When you deserve, you already have. I have an inheritance. Then I live up to it.

Director: An interesting distinction. I'm not sure it always holds, but I take your point. Aristocrats never earn. That's something the plebs do. Aristocrats strive to deserve what they've been given. And we'll never mind things like plebs striving to deserve a promotion they've been given.

Lawyer: We should mind those things—because they're a sign of worth.

69

Director: When aristocrats strive to deserve, who do they have in mind? Who has to believe they're worthy?

Lawyer: First of all, the aristocrat himself. Next, other aristocrats.

Director: What about the plebs?

Lawyer: There's danger there.

Director: What danger? What's wrong with the plebs thinking the aristocrats have what they deserve? I would have thought that would be the height of political excellence.

Lawyer: The danger is in pandering to the plebs. Of course it's fine for them to think we deserve what we have. But we cannot seek their approval.

Director: Because who are they to judge?

Lawyer: Exactly that. We only give weight to the opinions of the few.

Director: I prefer to give weight to the opinions that make sense.

Lawyer: No doubt there will be aristocrats who don't reason very well. But they will be the exception.

Director: Plebs often reason very well—especially on topics they're very familiar with.

Lawyer: But that's the thing. What are they familiar with? Mundane things.

Director: And aristocrats care about celestial things?

Lawyer: Don't be ridiculous. Aristocrats are concerned, above all else, with rule. With elevated, civilized rule.

Director: They rule themselves and they rule the plebs?

Lawyer: Ultimately, yes.

Director: Is there a sort of property right there?

Lawyer: What do you mean?

Director: Haven't you heard that popular phrase, 'I own you'? Can't the few say this to the many?

Lawyer: Why would they? Something you would own is something you like.

Director: And the plebs are beneath contempt?

Lawyer: Honestly? Yes, as a rule—but with the exceptions we've noted.

Director: Can someone have a property right in another? Can the aristocrats own the plebs?

Lawyer: That's a bad business.

Director: Why?

Lawyer: It's been done before and look where it went! Slavery is bad for everyone.

Director: What gave people the idea that they could own another?

Lawyer: Captives in war were considered property. The idea grew from there.

Director: The strong, the victorious own; the weak, the losers are owned.

Lawyer: That's the idea.

Director: Do you think that idea thrives though the idea of holding slaves is dead?

Lawyer: The idea that it's the strong that own? I do think that idea lives. It's just that strength is different today. A man who wouldn't survive a day in an army can be rich through his own efforts.

Director: Oh, I don't know. That same drive can be used to excel in many different things, including an army.

Lawyer: Well, you're right about drive. It's a certain set of the soul and mind. That makes someone strong.

Director: Aristocrats are trained from youth on up to achieve this drive. Yes?

Lawyer: Certainly. This drive and the fruits it brings make the few deserving of their wealth and position.

Director: They truly own what's theirs.

Lawyer: Yes, I like the way you put that. We have to take ownership of our lot.

Director: As do the plebs?

Lawyer: The successful plebs will. A sense of ownership for your life can take you far—even as a pleb.

70

Director: What does it mean to own ourselves?

Lawyer: What does it mean to own anything? You take responsibility for it.

Director: This is really how aristocrats think of everything they own? Your income from taxes on the plebs, you take responsibility for that?

Lawyer: Of course. It's on you to use the money wisely.

Director: Similarly, you have to use yourself, so to speak, wisely.

Lawyer: Yes, exactly that.

Director: A wise use of money is to be a good steward and conserve or make it grow. So a wise use of yourself is to conserve or make yourself grow.

Lawyer: And we all know which is best.

Director: Better spell it out for me.

Lawyer: It's best to grow.

Director: When money grows it becomes more of what it is. More money. When a human grows, can we say he becomes more of what he is? More human?

Lawyer: I like that definition. Human growth is excellence, what the few are all about.

Director: How does one become more human?

Lawyer: By gaining in virtue and knowledge.

Director: Virtue and knowledge, yes. With knowledge I suppose it's relatively easy to tell when there has been an increase. But virtue? Is that so easy to know?

Lawyer: Stand two people side by side and I think you'll be able to tell who has more virtue.

Director: We're using virtue in a very broad sense.

Lawyer: The broadest possible sense.

Director: Good. Because, you know, there's a way of thinking that says knowledge is virtue.

Lawyer: And I agree.

Director: But do you agree if we say virtue is knowledge?

Lawyer: We have to know how to carry ourselves. So, yes, virtue is knowledge. But it's not enough to know. You have to do. Aristocratic youth learn what virtue is. Anyone can learn what virtue is. But not anyone can live this virtue every day of their lives.

Director: With never a break?

Lawyer: With never a break.

Director: Is this what it means to own yourself?

Lawyer: To live yourself fully, every day. Yes.

Director: But why is virtue the fullness of life?

Lawyer: Why is knowledge the fullness of life?

Director: I didn't say it is.

Lawyer: But you're a philosopher.

Director: It seems I'm doomed to say this again and again. There's more to life than knowledge. But knowledge is the most we can own.

Lawyer: What are you saying? We can't own our virtuous actions?

Director: Those actions are owned by someone else.

Lawyer: What are you talking about?

Director: What is the essence of property?

Lawyer: Control.

Director: And you believe you control your virtuous actions.

Lawyer: Of course I do. Who else could?

Director: Those you seek to impress.

Lawyer: What if I'm seeking to impress myself?

Director: Suppose you lived alone on an island. Could your virtue impress yourself?

Lawyer: Well, there would be no one to interact with in virtuous fashion.

Director: And thus no virtue.

Lawyer: True, no virtue.

Director: So virtue depends on others.

Lawyer: I think you're twisting things a bit.

Director: How? No others, no virtue. Virtue depends on others.

Lawyer: Alright, I suppose that's fair.

Director: Do you control these others?

Lawyer: Do you mean do I rule them? No.

Director: Why not?

Lawyer: Because virtue is among equals.

Director: You need the opinion of others in order to have virtue. I mean, they have to believe in your virtue.

Lawyer: Of course.

71

Director: Can you control their belief?

Lawyer: No, but I have a very big say.

Director: Suppose you think you have your say, and you say; but no one responds in kind. What then?

Lawyer: Either I or they are lacking.

Director: Let's suppose they're lacking, and they simply fail to recognize your virtue. What do you do?

Lawyer: I hold fast.

Director: And let's suppose they aren't lacking. What then?

Lawyer: They would recognize my virtue.

Director: And if they don't?

Lawyer: I must be lacking. But that doesn't mean I'm their property.

Director: Doesn't it? No matter what you do, try as you might, you can't win them over to your virtue. Do you keep on trying? Or do you learn to satisfy them?

Lawyer: That's the act of a coward. If I did that, they would own my virtue.

Director: So here's the crux. Where do you take your bearings? From yourself or from them, your equals?

Lawyer: Always from myself.

Director: But you and your equals, you received the same education from earliest youth on up. No?

Lawyer: That's the idea in an aristocracy.

Director: So why do you differ over something so important? Virtue itself.

Lawyer: That's the problem with this hypothetical. We wouldn't differ so much. Sure, there will be slight differences of opinion. But nothing of a fundamental sort.

Director: So you own yourself.

Lawyer: I absolutely do.

Director: And if you don't, if you can't exercise your prerogative, that's the failure of the aristocracy.

Lawyer: That's a fatal flaw.

Director: So every aristocrat must own himself.

Lawyer: No doubt about that.

Director: And what about the plebs? Should they own themselves in this very same sense? Or is that too risky?

Lawyer: I... No. It's not too risky.

Director: There will be no ownership of any other human beings.

Lawyer: None.

Director: Alright. Everyone in this regime owns themselves. But what happens if they don't?

Lawyer: If it's an aristocrat, banishment.

Director: That's harsh.

Lawyer: The crime is serious.

Director: And if it happens in a pleb?

Lawyer: We'll let the plebs sort this out among themselves.

Director: Sounds good. You'll let these plebs do a lot of sorting out. Are you still thinking you'll rule them indirectly through their representatives?

Lawyer: Yes, until that no longer works.

Director: Hmm. But won't you own these representatives? Isn't that how the system works?

Lawyer: You have a point. More reason to migrate from indirect to direct rule of the plebs by the few.

72

Director: If you're going to rule the plebs, why not own them, too?

Lawyer: First of all, people would never go for that. Secondly, what good would it do us?

Director: Ownership means control. Isn't it easier to rule when you control?

Lawyer: The question isn't what's easier. The question is what's better.

Director: What's more important? The way you rule the plebs, or the way you rule your follow aristocrats?

Lawyer: The aristocrats.

Director: Why?

Lawyer: The plebs are easy to understand.

Director: Especially easy to understand when you own them.

Lawyer: Yes. But do you know why they're truly easy to understand?

Director: Tell me.

Lawyer: They lack sophistication.

Director: And aristocrats are rich in this.

Lawyer: None richer. If you want sophistication, look no further than any aristocratic culture that ever existed. You are guaranteed to find what you're looking for.

Director: I take it sophistication is part of excellence.

Lawyer: A very great part.

Director: Humor me and tell me what sophistication is.

Lawyer: Having a great deal of worldly experience. Knowing what to do with that experience.

Director: Can't plebs have a great deal of experience?

Lawyer: Not the full range. Pleb experience is more or less predictable. It's all the same. Aristocrats, however, are rich in experience. They see the world in all its highs and lows and everything in-between.

Director: If a born pleb were to see the world as you say, would that pleb gain sophistication?

Lawyer: No, absolutely not. It's almost the definition of pleb that you are incapable of processing all this information. The born aristocrat thrives on rich experience, revels in it. The pleb wants to go back to its mechanical work.

Director: Are you saying a born pleb and a born aristocrat are comfortable in different environments?

Lawyer: Absolutely yes! That may, in fact, be the definition of the two.

Director: This may be a bit trite, but are we saying the pleb watches local news and the aristocrat watches CNN?

Lawyer: I feel like you're trying to catch me up. But I'll answer yes, just the same. But think of local news as hyper local; and think of CNN as much more worldly than it is. Then we get the idea.

Director: The world of the pleb is small. The world of the aristocrat is vast.

Lawyer: Yes.

Director: But the world of the pleb is hundreds of millions. The world of the aristocrat is hundreds.

Lawyer: There is more true variety in the hundreds than there is in the hundreds of millions.

Director: What makes someone different?

Lawyer: Ways of thought.

Director: So the plebs all think alike?

Lawyer: When push comes to shove, yes.

Director: And the aristocrats vary in their thinking?

Lawyer: About certain things, no. But about all the rest? As varied as you can imagine.

Director: Why is that?

Lawyer: Plebs are all concerned with the basic needs of life. Aristocrats have those basic needs met—so they can branch out and explore other fields.

73

Director: What do they do once they've explored?

Lawyer: They share with their peers.

Director: So someone might write a play?

Lawyer: Of course. That's a fine way to share sophisticated knowledge of the world.

Director: But do they just give it away?

Lawyer: What do you mean?

Director: To their peers. Is everyone free to make whatever use of it they might?

Lawyer: I suppose. But what are you driving at?

Director: You really don't know? You, the specialist in intellectual property?

Lawyer: But here's the thing. There's no need for that in an aristocracy.

Director: Why not?

Lawyer: What is intellectual property, the idea of intellectual property, supposed to do?

Director: Encourage people to think profitable thoughts.

Lawyer: You put that very well. Well, the few don't need to turn a profit on their thoughts. Pride in thought is enough. The playwright doesn't need a nickel for his work. Admiration is enough.

Director: And it's the same with things that would otherwise be patents?

Lawyer: Esteem is the coin of the realm.

Director: I'm impressed. So you're saying there is no such thing as intellectual property when things are right.

Lawyer: Share, share, and share alike. That's what we do.

Director: But not with the plebs?

Lawyer: I'm not sure. On the one hand, this might be one of the many benefits of being a pleb in our age. On the other hand, would they understand?

Director: Maybe you'd use these works of the mind for propaganda purposes.

Lawyer: I prefer sympathy building to propaganda.

Director: How would a pleb come to sympathize with the nobles.

Lawyer: Some plebs are not born plebs. Some have aristocratic traits. We must identify these youths and expose them to our ideas, our works. Once exposed we have an ally for life.

Director: That's it? You let them see a play and they're sold for life?

Lawyer: You'd be surprised what passing honors win.

Director: But aren't you just getting their hopes up only to be dashed?

Lawyer: I'm not saying they can marry into the aristocracy. But we do need librarians, set designers, musicians—you name it. These jobs will bring them close to what they admire. And that can be enough.

Director: Are you saying you bring the best and brightest into service of the aristocracy? And they will willingly come?

Lawyer: Yes. But woe to us if we fail to deal with those who don't willingly come.

Director: Those who are loyal to their class.

Lawyer: Yes. They are trouble in the making.

Director: Because they have been exposed, but don't recognize the superiority of the few. What will you do with them?

Lawyer: Send them into exile. The second harshest penalty there is.

Director: The harshest is death, I assume. But won't there be prisons? Is exile worse than that? Exile might be a relief.

Lawyer: And secretly the aristocrats might want to give them that.

Director: Because aristocrats value loyalty, even misguided loyalty.

Lawyer: Like no one else does.

Director: Why do you think that is?

Lawyer: Because when you are a very small class against a very great many, you need to stick together.

Director: Against?

Lawyer: You know what I mean.

Director: I didn't know you could be against something you own.

74

Lawyer: We cannot, will not, own them.

Director: Why?

Lawyer: Because who wants to own what they don't like?

Director: It's as simple as that?

Lawyer: Yes.

Director: Property must be something we like.

Lawyer: Well, it only makes sense, don't you think?

Director: I suppose if you find yourself owning something you don't like, you just—disown it.

Lawyer: And we'll disown the plebs.

Director: Those poor plebs. What can they own?

Lawyer: Anything and everything they own today. That's the genius of our system.

Director: And the aristocrats can own everything they own today, too.

Lawyer: Yes. The only thing that changes is rule.

Director: No small thing. Who wants to be ruled?

Lawyer: There are some who do, you know.

Director: Do you look down on them?

Lawyer: Do I look down on those who like what we do? I don't know. Yes, I suppose.

Director: I would think you'd be better disposed toward those who like what you do, which is what you are. Do you admire those who hate you and your rule?

Lawyer: I'd prefer to avoid that situation entirely. Remember, we come to power after catastrophe. Not many are going to hate us for saving them from the wreckage of the former regime.

Director: So you expect gratitude?

Lawyer: A grateful nation is best.

Director: And you really have no intent to grow super rich?

Lawyer: No, just rich enough.

Director: Why not super rich?

Lawyer: Because at a certain point the money owns you.

Director: You want just enough for a clearly defined purpose.

Lawyer: Yes, and if a family squirrels away money we will take it back. Money is meant to be spent.

Director: Because otherwise it owns you.

Lawyer: Yes.

Director: But you are, of course, depending on a set income from taxes on the plebs.

Lawyer: That's the only way.

Director: The income is your property, the fact of the annual levy.

Lawyer: Yes, but it's more than property. It's our right.

75

Director: Do you believe people must have a right to property, or can anyone own?

Lawyer: In today's society anyone can own. And for the plebs of the future it will be that way, too. But for us? The few? We must have a right.

Director: Your excellence.

Lawyer: Yes.

Director: Excellence justifies ownership.

Lawyer: Well, I don't like the notion of justification. It makes it sound like we're doing something wrong. Owning is right, not wrong.

Director: Owning is right, or is a right?

Lawyer: What's the difference, Director? If we deserve what we own, all is right.

Director: But how do you know you deserve? Is it enough if your fellow aristocrats say you do? Or maybe it's enough if the plebs say you do?

Lawyer: What do you think?

Director: Most people rely on some sort of theory to tell them they're right. Do you want a theory?

Lawyer: I'm distrustful of theories. All aristocrats are distrustful of theories.

Director: Why do you think that is?

Lawyer: I can tell you why I distrust theories. They're usually part of some agenda.

Director: And you have no agenda.

Lawyer: Nothing other than human excellence.

Director: But doesn't that just push the problem further back? How do you know what's excellent?

Lawyer: I don't want any sort of theoretical bar we need to reach. Excellence is self-evident to those who care for it.

Director: Do you really believe there are people who don't care for excellence?

Lawyer: It's not a matter of belief. Look at most of the plebs. They believe excellence is something like being good at your job, or providing spectacular entertainment for when the work is done.

Director: But don't aristocrats want to be excellent at their job of rule?

Lawyer: Rule is a unique phenomenon. It's not like being an excellent pizza chef.

Director: It's nobler.

Lawyer: Yes, certainly. Rule is the ultimate in nobility. That's what nobles do.

Director: Aside from being excellent.

Lawyer: It's fine if you want to tease.

Director: No, I'm being serious. I really want to know what this excellence is.

Lawyer: It's holding the right standards of human interaction and living up to them.

Director: Name a standard.

Lawyer: Honesty.

Director: Plebs aren't honest?

Lawyer: Oh, plebs can be as honest as the day is long.

Director: What's the difference?

Lawyer: The degree to which one can be honest—to extremes.

Director: Plebs can be honest to extremes. What's special about aristocratic honesty?

Lawyer: They have more to be honest about.

Director: What does that mean? Are you talking about their rich life experience?

Lawyer: That's exactly what I'm talking about.

Director: Okay. What's another standard?

Lawyer: Integrity.

Director: How does that differ from honesty?

Lawyer: Integrity is when your deeds match your words.

76

Director: Plebs can't do that? Match their deeds to their words?

Lawyer: Yes, but what's the quality of the words?

Director: Aristocrats are more daring?

Lawyer: Infinitely.

Director: Maybe we've hit on the quality par excellence of the aristocrat.

Lawyer: Yes, maybe we have. Infinite daring, when backed up, is excellence.

Director: Infinite daring, all of a piece.

Lawyer: You know, Director, we really are on to something here.

Director: Yes, we do seem to be on to something. What does it mean for daring to be infinite?

Lawyer: It's unbounded. By that I mean that no boundary stops it.

Director: Is this daring in thought or in deed?

Lawyer: Either. Both. Daring in thought can lead to daring in deed. Daring in deed can lead to daring in thought. The daring is the thing.

Director: But I have to ask—can't plebs dare in either or?

Lawyer: Plebs can dare. But they don't have resources it takes to really dare.

Director: Resources? Physical? Mental? Property?

Lawyer: All three.

Director: Property I can understand. It gives you a platform of safety from which to dare.

Lawyer: No, that's not it at all!

Director: Okay, okay. Let's talk about physical resources.

Lawyer: We may as well talk about physical and mental resources together. They are, essentially, the same.

Director: You're saying the mental is physical.

Lawyer: Yes. Biochemistry has proven that to my satisfaction.

Director: So what advantage do aristocrats have?

Lawyer: It's in the blood. They come from a long line of daring.

Director: Can you pinpoint what it is that allows one to dare?

Lawyer: I'm going to fall back on integrity here. There is a deep integrity between body and mind that only aristocrats achieve.

Director: Is it a sort of tension?

Lawyer: Exactly that. Aristocrats bear tremendous tension successfully. And yes, there are certain plebs who might be able to do this under different, more supportive circumstances.

Director: Aristocrats are supported?

Lawyer: Everyone needs a little support. Aristocrats support one another. They are all kin of sorts.

Director: Kin in ownership, yes.

Lawyer: What do you mean?

Director: What you own affects who you are. You take on certain traits from certain forms of property. Since all of you aristocrats will own income streams from taxes on the plebs, you will have certain traits in common.

Lawyer: What traits?

Director: Concern for the welfare and productivity of the plebs.

Lawyer: True enough. But that's not the only reason we'll care. We want to rule well.

Director: Yes, sure. But wouldn't you agree the property interest enhances that desire?

Lawyer: I agree. But aside from that, we own the same sort of things as the plebs. Homes, cars, furniture, and so on—just of a nicer variety.

Director: The nicer variety of the property will affect you in subtle and not so subtle ways. It will reinforce your sense of superiority.

Lawyer: Well, that goes without saying.

Director: And the poorer quality of the property of the plebs will reinforce their sense of inferiority in comparison with you.

Lawyer: True.

77

Director: And what about their jobs?

Lawyer: What about them?

Director: Won't they be a mark of inferiority?

Lawyer: Of course they will.

Director: The aristocrats won't have jobs. Yes, they'll rule, and maybe hold certain posts—but that doesn't amount to a job.

Lawyer: No doubt.

Director: Will the plebs view their jobs as property, much in the sense you view your income from taxes as property?

Lawyer: Well, this gets at a bigger problem.

Director: How so?

Lawyer: We aristocrats will sit atop the pleb economy, which is basically today's economy but with the super rich cut out.

Director: Will anyone be more wealthy than the aristocrats?

Lawyer: I just don't see how we can allow it. So we either have a high ceiling for ourselves, or we cut down the money the upper echelon of plebs can earn.

Director: Do you worry that will weaken the economy and thus your base of support?

Lawyer: I do. What truly creative soul will strive no end to be merely at the head of the plebs?

Director: Are you forgetting what you said? You would tease the plebs with hopes of one day cracking into the aristocracy. And if not that, honors can be given. A little honor can go a very long way.

Lawyer: It's true. And honors from those who truly know excellence go even further.

Director: Then maybe you have nothing to worry about with the economy.

Lawyer: I think you have a point. The aristocrats can quickly settle thorny business disputes that would otherwise drag out in the courts for years. Labor disputes would be a thing of the past.

Director: Because you'd always side with management?

Lawyer: No, I think we'd often side with labor. It all depends on who is being reasonable. Aristocrats respect that quality no end.

Director: Because aristocrats value domestic tranquility no end.

Lawyer: Well, yes. But the plebs value that, too.

Director: Sounds like it might be a good system—if you can manage to somehow kill a free people's pride.

Lawyer: We're talking about a post-free state that leads to the aristocracy. I thought I made that clear. A free people would never allow an aristocracy in.

Director: So the aristocracy marks an improvement?

Lawyer: Of course it does. But don't smirk at me like that.

Director: Sorry. I was just thinking that aristocracy is such a great thing that you can only allow it once your spirit is broken.

Lawyer: The aristocrats' spirits never broke, even through the calamities that crushed the plebs.

Director: So these aristocrats were once free democrats?

Lawyer: The freest of the free. And they will be freer still once they are acknowledged as the ruling few.

Director: What is it about rule that makes one free? I thought rule was a burden.

Lawyer: Don't you know? Freedom is a burden when exercised right.

Director: Can you explain?

Lawyer: Freedom and pride are intertwined. In order to be proud, you have to do things worthy of pride. These things aren't easy. That's the sense in which freedom is a burden.

Director: With freedom comes responsibility.

Lawyer: Yes, exactly that.

Director: And aristocrats are worthy of the greatest responsibilities.

Lawyer: You understand.

78

Director: And I think I have an inkling why they are so prepared.

Lawyer: Why?

Director: They are the property of their parents until they reach majority.

Lawyer: It's true! More so than with the plebs. Aristocratic parents can be severe—because they expect so much.

Director: Plebeian parents are more affectionate?

Lawyer: Oh, definitely. They often treat their children as friends. At least they are friendly with their kids. Note how they often call them 'buddy'. My parents wouldn't dream of ever calling me that.

Director: They put a lot of pressure on you.

Lawyer: To prepare me for life. Yes. And they deserve, for all their efforts, respect.

Director: Plebs don't respect their parents?

Lawyer: Not the way aristocrats do.

Director: Could that be because aristocrat parents can disinherit their children? Can they do that in your regime?

Lawyer: I'm not going to lie. It's an important factor in a young aristocrat's life. No one wants to lose their inheritance. But this fear introduces a certain healthy discipline. Parents need this control to bring out their children's best. So, yes, parents can disinherit in our regime.

Director: What happens to the disinherited? Are they banished, too?

Lawyer: I don't see how they couldn't be. After all, what would they do to support themselves? Work like a pleb? No, we'd have to send them away.

Director: With enough to support themselves on.

Lawyer: Of course. Not extravagantly, but comfortably enough.

Director: Enough what?

Lawyer: That they don't cause trouble.

Director: I see. And the inheritance goes to the next in line. Will you encourage your aristocrats to have many children?

Lawyer: That's totally up to them.

Director: But with more of them there will be less money to go round. Over a couple of generations you could have scores of impoverished few. How do you deal with this? Raise taxes on the plebs?

Lawyer: It's a problem, as you say. Maybe we need to limit births to two per couple.

Director: Yes, that's probably wise. If the aristocracy grows top-heavy there will be trouble both with themselves and the plebs. Do you think people will object?

Lawyer: I think they'll see the wisdom in this.

Director: Will it be a law? Or maybe just a an understood thing.

Lawyer: It will be an understood thing.

Director: What happens to violators?

Lawyer: Director, we don't have to have this all figured out now. It's good we're thinking about it. But we can only go so far here today.

Director: Of course. After all, how to handle this will be determined by the few who rule, not some philosopher and his friend over dinner.

79

Lawyer: Yes, I think we've said enough about property for now.

Director: Yes, but I think we've only scratched the surface.

Lawyer: How so?

Director: Have you ever heard 'property' used to mean an attribute, quality, or characteristic?

Lawyer: You mean like the properties of gold?

Director: Sure, things like that. Do you think there's a relation to property in our earlier sense?

Lawyer: Well, there's a bridge. In Italian we find the root of property in *proprio*, which means one's own.

Director: And that derives, of course, from the Latin.

Lawyer: Yes.

Director: Wealth belongs to, properly, the aristocrats—the best.

Lawyer: Exactly so.

Director: Wealth is an attribute of the best.

Lawyer: It is.

Director: To the best, wealth is one's own.

Lawyer: I like what you're saying. It's all of a piece.

Director: And if one has one's own, one's proper things, life is as it should be.

Lawyer: Yes.

Director: But lacking one's own, life is... what?

Lawyer: Unjust.

Director: Because you don't have what you deserve.

Lawyer: Correct.

Director: People often disagree on what they all deserve. Do you think they disagree on what belongs properly to an aristocrat?

Lawyer: I think people agree on this. But they question who is truly among the few.

Director: If many think they're among the few, there are no few.

Lawyer: Not quite. There can be a few, but they are under pressure.

Director: It's best that the many agree that the few are the few?

Lawyer: That's like saying it's best in logic for A to be A.

Director: So the question is who is an aristocrat. What makes an aristocrat what he is? What are the attributes, qualities, and characteristics of an aristocrat?

Lawyer: We've been talking about this all along.

Director: Yes, but we've been rather... vague.

Lawyer: Look, this isn't a science. It's something you know when you see it.

Director: Because aristocrats are known by their looks? Tall, well-shaped, elegant, strong?

Lawyer: You want to paint me as shallow.

Director: No, I want to know what you think.

Lawyer: I think aristocrats are made that way. What's wrong with perfect human form?

Director: Nothing. But perfect for what?

Lawyer: Liking how you're made.

Director: The plebs don't like how they're made?

Lawyer: Oh, they have a certain creature comfort with themselves. But they're jealous of us. Who wants to be short when others are tall? And so on.

Director: So what happens if two of the few give birth to one short of stature?

Lawyer: It's unfortunate for him, the short one. But he'll make up for it in other things.

Director: Things like rule. A Napoleon of sorts.

Lawyer: Well, not to that extreme—but yes.

80

Director: What are the properties of a non-extreme Napoleonic aristocrat?

Lawyer: You're basically asking what are the non-physical properties of any aristocrat? That's what we've been talking about today.

Director: Yes, but....

Lawyer: Character counts above all else. You must be trustworthy yet capable of maneuver, frank yet tactful, of integrity yet flexible, bold yet reserved, cold yet passionate. In other words, you must be 'just so' in so many things.

Director: But that's the thing. When we think of aristocrats we think of people who are 'just so'. But just so what?

Lawyer: Excellent.

Director: What is a mark of excellence so we can recognize it.

Lawyer: Success in rule.

Director: And how do we succeed in rule?

Lawyer: Through achieving internal peace and lack of external interference.

Director: Maybe that's the mark of an aristocrat. A person who has internal peace and lacks external interference.

Lawyer: You know, I think you're on to something there. An upright man. That's what an aristocrat is.

Director: What about an upright pleb?

Lawyer: Possibly a unlucky born aristocrat—someone we'd take an interest in.

Director: So out go the bad aristocrats and in come the good plebs?

Lawyer: Something like that. But infrequently, or else there's trouble.

Director: You don't want property to change hands too often.

Lawyer: No, we don't. We need stability.

Director: Why?

Lawyer: That's the primary end of good rule.

Director: Okay, buy why is it the end?

Lawyer: It allows for the full development of character. It encourages character formation and growth. Chaos makes you jittery and not a full man.

Director: And there is more chaos among the plebs than among the few.

Lawyer: Infinitely more. Everyone there is on the make. No one is on the make among the few.

Director: Because they have a secure financial future from the time they are born.

Lawyer: That goes a long way. Without that in the forefront of our minds, we can't concentrate on character.

Director: And virtue goes hand in hand with character.

Lawyer: The two are essentially one and the same.

Director: Do the jittery have virtue?

Lawyer: Well, they can work a good con, etcetera. But they don't have virtue in the proper sense.

Director: The virtue that comes from money.

Lawyer: There's an important distinction here. The virtue doesn't come from money; money allows the virtue to form.

Director: That's cutting it pretty thin, if you ask me.

Lawyer: No, really. Money doesn't make the man. The man makes himself, thanks to money. Can't you see the difference?

Director: I suppose I can. Until I really can, I'll take it from you on trust.

81

Lawyer: You can have money and not be the man you might be.

Director: And you can be the man and not have money?

Lawyer: No, it doesn't work that way. Lack of money will eventually wear you down, though you can make a good show for a while.

Director: You really feel no shame for being dependent?

Lawyer: Do I feel shame for needing to eat? Of course not. Do I feel shame for needing money in order to live a certain way? No. These are just the facts of life. Ask any pleb.

Director: They'll tell me the few can only be what they are because of their wealth.

Lawyer: Yes, they certainly will. And they're right. But they make a common mistake. They assume that given money, they could be that way, too.

Director: It takes training from early youth.

Lawyer: It does. Give a pleb an inheritance and watch him become a boor. He wouldn't know how to become an aristocrat if his life depended on it.

Director: But there are exceptions?

Lawyer: As we've said. But you have to catch them early enough so they don't wear themselves out. But, also, not too early. They have to prove their traits.

Director: What's a sign?

Lawyer: Of a born aristocrat stuck with the plebs? He can cut a pleb down with a look.

Director: How does that work?

Lawyer: There's a certain superiority all plebs can sense. It's a show of inner strength.

Director: Inner ruthlessness.

Lawyer: Yes. A willingness to destroy if tested.

Director: And basically people are afraid to call the bluff.

Lawyer: Oh, it's no bluff. That's why the look cuts people down. You rarely see this look on someone's face. But when you do, you know.

Director: What is it? A sort of instinct warning you to stand down?

Lawyer: Yes, that's exactly it.

Director: What happens if an aristocrat uses this look on another aristocrat?

Lawyer: The other will laugh—because he's willing, too.

Director: And plebs? Can they give the look?

Lawyer: No, and it's hard to explain why.

Director: Try.

Lawyer: You need a certain elevation, an unshakable sense of superiority. That's what backs the look. Plebs almost never have an unshakable sense of superiority. And when they do, they often become criminals or die some tragic death.

Director: Would an aristocrat laugh when exposed to the look of a pleb?

Lawyer: My goodness would he ever! Out of joy!

Director: Joy?

Lawyer: In recognition of kin.

Director: Even if it were a criminal?

Lawyer: Even so. Sometimes circumstances can force a man into a life of crime.

Director: Would the aristocrat seek to elevate this man to the few?

Lawyer: Not at once, no. It's not that simple. He might just laugh and then turn and walk away, leaving the other to his own devices.

Director: How would the pleb react to this response?

Lawyer: He, too, would recognize kin. And that might give him a great deal of food for thought.

82

Director: I suppose an aristocrat might give the withering look to another aristocrat in order to test his mettle.

Lawyer: Yes, if there's doubt about someone, this means can be employed.

Director: And if the person in question doesn't laugh or show a similar sign of worth?

Lawyer: It's a sign that we need to scrutinize his dealings.

Director: All from a look.

Lawyer: Looks are telling. But like I said, we need to look into him further. Nothing more for the time being, but nothing less.

Director: Aristocrats constantly test one another, don't they?

Lawyer: They do, but in more subtle ways. We hold each other to very high standards.

Director: Doesn't that get tiring?

Lawyer: That's why we need the resources that allow us privacy.

Director: I was wondering about that. I thought aristocrats were always sort of, well, you know—spying on one another.

Lawyer: That's only when an aristocracy starts to go bad. In a healthy aristocracy, people have plenty of private time to pursue their interests.

Director: Philosophy, or history, or music, or whatever?

Lawyer: Yes, whatever.

Director: What if an aristocrat likes plebeian culture—comic books, say?

Lawyer: Let him study them to his heart's content. We'll have an expert on pleb culture this way.

Director: And that can only help you rule. Is there anything you can't turn to your advantage?

Lawyer: One thing. The belief that aristocracy is fundamentally unjust.

Director: How does an aristocrat become convinced of that?

Lawyer: Love affairs.

Director: What do you mean?

Lawyer: When an aristocrat falls in love with a pleb, trouble is afoot.

Director: What do you do? Prevent such relationships?

Lawyer: I wish we could. There can be no intermarriage. But love? Very hard to prevent.

Director: Do you think there's something wrong with an aristocrat who falls in love with a pleb?

Lawyer: No. I can see how it happens. I actually sympathize here.

Director: So what do you do?

Lawyer: Nothing. Let the relationship be. But if questions of justice bubble up, we warn our aristocratic friend that continued speech like this will result in banishment.

Director: There is no freedom of speech, as I think you said before.

Lawyer: I did. And there is no freedom here because we have an aristocracy to run.

Director: But what about other topics, those not having to do with the regime?

Lawyer: Complete and utter freedom.

Director: Crass talk, vulgarities, irreverences?

Lawyer: Yes, all those things are fine.

Director: But irreverence toward the regime?

Lawyer: You're talking about comedies? Comedies are fine. They sometimes help correct mistakes. But there is a question of tone.

Director: Lighthearted works well; caustic fails?

Lawyer: Precisely. Sarcasm is a vice we cannot tolerate.

Director: I thought aristocrats were eminently sarcastic.

Lawyer: And they are—in a failing regime. Sarcasm is a vice.

Director: Tell me why.

Lawyer: Because it's a sign of weakness. The powerful have no need for sarcasm. Only the weak.

83

Director: Are you basically saying that in an aristocracy, weakness is a vice?

Lawyer: I am saying that. Aristocrats must be strong.

Director: And what do you do with the weak? Banish them, too?

Lawyer: If they were the head of their house, I would prefer to take their status and give it to another more worthy within the family.

Director: By worthy you mean powerful.

Lawyer: Yes.

Director: Haven't you heard that power corrupts?

Lawyer: Not in aristocracies it doesn't.

Director: Why not?

Lawyer: Because every head of house is powerful. Call it a check if you like.

Director: And aristocracy rots when that power decays.

Lawyer: It does. And then the weeds grow strong.

Director: The weeds that strangle the flowers of the aristocracy.

Lawyer: Yes. And then the few are forced to spend their time fighting the weeds, not striving for higher accomplishments.

Director: What happens to the plebs when an aristocracy decays?

Lawyer: What happens to anyone when rule grows bad? They suffer. And they long for the good old days of the few in command. But let's not talk about this.

Director: What shall we talk about?

Lawyer: Education.

Director: Why that?

Lawyer: Because many snobs value education above all else. They think there is an aristocracy of the educated.

Director: What's wrong with thinking that? Isn't there?

Lawyer: There is in the minds of the plebs. And only some of the plebs. They see education as a way out of the limits of plebeian life. They long for their children to go to the top schools.

Director: Don't they learn in these schools?

Lawyer: They do. But often they learn mere propaganda, and how to spew it themselves.

Director: What kind of education will aristocrats receive, higher education I mean? Will they have their own schools?

Lawyer: Of course they will. Do you think pleb and aristocrat can learn together? But here's the important thing. Aristocrats are secure in their place. Education to them is a tool to enhance their thinking.

Director: But with the plebs?

Lawyer: They view education as a means to climb. This overvalues and cheapens the education at once. Does that make sense?

Director: It does. So what will you do about plebeian schools?

Lawyer: Limit them to trade schools. Mechanics, doctors, lawyers, software engineers, and so on—all will be considered members of a trade. No more and no less.

Director: What about entrepreneurs?

Lawyer: Members of the business trade.

Director: So the plebs are essentially tradesmen.

Lawyer: All of them, yes.

Director: And none of the aristocrats will practice a trade.

Lawyer: Not a one. Trade debases. Can you see how that is?

Director: I can, compared to a life of leisure and rule.

Lawyer: How about compared to a life of philosophy?

Director: Philosophy doesn't compare itself to other ways of life.

Lawyer: Oh, that's nonsense. Of course it does. We all compare ourselves to see where we stand.

Director: Philosophy is other.

Lawyer: What, it stands on a completely different plane?

Director: It constantly questions where it stands. That means it could never stand on equal footing with aristocrats.

Lawyer: Or plebs for that matter.

Director: Just so. Philosophers sometimes feel they're above the aristocrats; and sometimes they feel they're below the plebs—and sometimes at the same time.

Lawyer: Isn't that an exhausting way to live? Don't you want to know your place and keep to it?

Director: I do when I can.

Lawyer: Why can't you always keep to your place?

Director: Philosophy drags me away.

84

Lawyer: What do you mean it drags you away? Is philosophy a thug?

Director: I wouldn't say that. I'd say it's very insistent.

Lawyer: I've read plenty of philosophy. And every time it starts insisting I close the book. After all, who is some philosopher to insist?

Director: A point well taken. But I feel a certain sympathy for these philosophers. A suggestion from one of them is like a command. I must obey.

Lawyer: Why? What's the point?

Director: To see where it leads. I find nothing more exciting.

Lawyer: You're talking about thinking in a different direction?

Director: I knew you'd understand.

Lawyer: I can understand that. But I don't find that terribly exciting.

Director: You find command exciting.

Lawyer: Ruling, yes. It gets my blood pumping.

Director: Well, daring thoughts get my blood pumping. We're just different in this way. But I don't see how daring thoughts would get in the way of rule. In fact, they might enhance rule.

Lawyer: Yes, but I can't go down every crazy rabbit hole some philosopher suggests. Rule takes a steady hand.

Director: Of course it does. But it also takes a certain amount of creativity. You can read and disregard what you take as crazy ideas while pulling out the best.

Lawyer: I'm surprised you say that.

Director: Why? What do you mean?

Lawyer: You once told me that a work of philosophy is a sort of whole. You can't pick and choose what you like. One part informs another. That's what you said.

Director: Yes, but things were different then. It wasn't clear to me that you were moving into the aristocracy. What's good for the goose isn't good for the gander.

Lawyer: Am I the goose or the gander?

Director: You are the goose who lays the golden egg. That egg is called a thriving regime.

Lawyer: So you do think my rule will be good for the plebs.

Director: What are the alternatives? A democracy collapsed into mob rule? A tyrant seizing control? Your aristocracy is wonderful by comparison. The best of all the available bad regimes. But there is one thing.

Lawyer: Of course there is.

Director: If the democracy is really doing so badly, how good can its economy be? You know, the economy that supports your class.

Lawyer: Economies can bounce back quickly when conditions are right.

Director: You have more faith than I do.

Lawyer: People will be starved for good work. A command and control economy can give them that quickly. Look at how quickly the economy turned around after the Great Depression.

Director: Because of a massive war.

Lawyer: Well, who says we might not need another war?

Director: And aristocrats will lead the way.

Lawyer: This will be the transition period when everything gels.

Director: You might be right. That might be what it takes. The best of many bad options.

Lawyer: But the best nonetheless.

Director: Would you say that about yourself and your peers? The best of many deeply flawed people?

Lawyer: No, I'd prefer not to say that. To focus on the flaws is a mistake. Consider the plebs. I'd like the plebs to be as good as they can. It forces us to up our game. Haven't you ever heard that good competition raises the playing level of the better team? Or that poor competition lowers that level?

Director: I have heard that and think there's truth therein. So you'll improve the lives of the plebs and trust their virtue will improve.

Lawyer: Yes. The plebs can have their virtue and we will have excellence.

Director: And virtue, too.

Lawyer: Of course—but in the Renaissance sense.

Director: And for our viewers at home who don't know what that is?

Lawyer: What Machiavelli values in a prince.

85

Director: So your aristocracy will consist of various princes?

Lawyer: Yes, each will rule in his own sphere—his family estate. All will rule each other and the plebs.

Director: Interesting. We went from annual income from taxes to estates.

Lawyer: What do you think the annual income is for?

Director: Won't there be competition for the greatest estate? Or will you practice equality here?

Lawyer: Ah, you've brought us to the crux. I believe the income should be the same for all—even those who hold high positions of responsibility.

Director: So the estates are all relatively the same?

Lawyer: Well, people will start out with different amounts of wealth, and they'll pass it on to their kids. I don't think we should interfere with that.

Director: So the estates will differ.

Lawyer: Yes.

Director: Are you worried about this as a source of jealousy?

Lawyer: I'm certainly concerned about jealousy, but I think we'll be okay.

Director: You'll be too busy ruling the world to care.

Lawyer: Right.

Director: What does it take to rule the world?

Lawyer: Virtue and force.

Director: Let's assume you have the virtue. Where do you get the force?

Lawyer: From the military. Where else?

Director: Supposing there's a great transition-making war, how will you control the military? Why won't it take over?

Lawyer: Well, in a sense it will.

Director: I don't understand.

Lawyer: The highest ranking military leaders will be brought on as aristocrats.

Director: And you'll keep the basic command structure beneath them intact.

Lawyer: Right.

Director: These leaders used to answer to the president. To whom do they answer now?

Lawyer: We'll have some sort of war council. Being chosen for this council will be one of the highest honors in the land.

Director: I'm sure it will be. But what happens when one of these original military leaders grows old and dies? Is his position inherited by his son? What if he has no son? What if the son isn't as competent as the father?

Lawyer: We promote from within the military.

Director: From the plebs. Interesting. So these men elevated to the aristocracy, will they have a fully inheritable estate, or will it be for their lives only?

Lawyer: Well, it's a bit of problem. If the estate is not inheritable, what becomes of the offspring? Do we send them back to the plebs? But if we keep them on among the few, our numbers will keep on growing.

Director: While the tax base remains the same.

Lawyer: Yes. I don't have the answer. We'll have to cross that bridge when we come to it.

Director: Agreed. But if the population and economy of the plebs keep on growing, you might have your answer.

Lawyer: A good economy will likely cause the population to grow.

Director: More heads to tax. The business experts among the aristocracy will have their hands full.

Lawyer: Indeed they will. I expect if we win the war we'll see a boom.

Director: High time to reward those fighting chiefs.

Lawyer: There is one more problem, however.

Director: Oh? What is it?

Lawyer: What if the highest ranking general is a true-to-heart pleb?

Director: And he still wants into the aristocracy?

Lawyer: Yes. What then? Can we refuse? Choose someone else?

Director: I don't know. You certainly don't want to upset the excellence of the few. Maybe you leave him in place? Say he's too valuable to move and reward him with an income stream?

Lawyer: And when someone beneath him in rank is chosen for the few? How will he react?

Director: Maybe you have to give him a very big income stream to make up for that.

Lawyer: We're not going to be in the business of bribing our generals. We'll just have to select the one beneath him and tell the general-pleb too bad.

Director: And if he complains?

Lawyer: We crush him without mercy. We have to stamp this sort of thing out.

Director: That's the spirit. I'll leave the details to you. But, you know, you might have the same sort of problem in business or other fields of endeavor. Do you admit the people who do so well to your ranks?

Lawyer: We might. More reason to keep our birth rate low.

Director: But don't aristocrats traditionally like big families?

Lawyer: Traditionally everyone likes big families. We can encourage this in the plebs, but not among the aristocracy. The few must stay few.

Director: What if money were no problem?

Lawyer: Money is always a problem.

Director: Even for you in your new regime?

Lawyer: It's not a problem if we limit ourselves to two children. More than that, there's trouble. That's all I mean.

Director: How well will your children come to know the plebs?

Lawyer: I don't think we should expose them to them until they've had a chance to mature.

Director: You want the plebs to be other.

Lawyer: They are other. It's not a matter of what I want.

Director: Then why not expose your children to them earlier on?

Lawyer: I don't want them to develop affections for them.

Director: Why not?

Lawyer: It's hard to make clear eyed ruling decisions when your heart gets in the way.

Director: What sort of affections do you have in mind?

Lawyer: Think of the way a boy loves his dog.

Director: That can be a very fierce love.

Lawyer: Well, that's the kind of love we simply can't afford.

Director: You don't want judgment to be colored by love.

Lawyer: Judgment needs to be clear.

Director: In fact, you're not particularly concerned about love in your marriages, either. Are you?

Lawyer: Oh, there can be love. But that's not the point. Stability of the regime is what counts. Two friends in a marriage in a stable regime can find satisfaction in life. You have to be practical here, Director.

Director: Love takes a back seat to rule.

Lawyer: Yes, it does. Because without proper rule, there is no love that lasts.

87

Director: So love to you is not a boiling passion.

Lawyer: It's a passion, but one that simmers. And I'd rather have a simmer for my whole life than a boil that lasts only a while.

Director: How do you know the boil will only last a while?

Lawyer: Because all the water evaporates quickly, my friend. It's in the nature of things.

Director: What about a boil that settles into a simmer?

Lawyer: Prove to me that it's a simmer and I'm on board.

Director: If your children had boiling loves, with no sign of simmer, you'd break the loves off?

Lawyer: I would, hate me though they might. I'd do it because it's best for them.

Director: And the regime.

Lawyer: The regime is what brings out their best. But let me tell you something. If I had my way even the simmers would be gone.

Director: You want the marriage of friends.

Lawyer: I do. It's more stable this way.

Director: But you're not talking about loveless marriages.

Lawyer: No, I'm certainly not. The love of friends is a wonderful thing. A powerful thing. An enduring thing.

Director: Until along comes a boil.

Lawyer: We have to be like Odysseus and lash ourselves to the mast of our ship.

Director: Or indulge the boil on the sly, until it goes away?

Lawyer: No.

Director: Is boiling love beneath you?

Lawyer: What?

Director: Is it beneath you to be head over heels in love?

Lawyer: Yes, as a matter of fact—it is. It's one thing to feel it. It's another thing to act on it. It's a plebeian belief, you know.

Director: What is?

Lawyer: That love is the most important thing in the world. It's not. Excellence is.

Director: If you are excellent, love is beneath you?

Lawyer: Oh, you make it sound so bad. But for that kind of love? The answer is yes.

Director: Is there anything above you?

Lawyer: Why, no. That's the whole point. An aristocrat fully committed to excellence is the most noble thing in the world. There is nothing higher.

Director: You don't have ideals?

Lawyer: We do. But they are tools, not ends.

Director: You don't have gods?

Lawyer: The time for that is past.

Director: Nothing above you but the stars in the sky. That's tempting.

Lawyer: Isn't it? I find the prospect thrilling.

Director: What's above the plebs?
Lawyer: We are.

Director: Besides the few, what do they hold above them?

Lawyer: Love, as we said. Probably some sort of god. Hope.

Director: That they'll one day join the aristocracy?

Lawyer: Or serve as our lieutenants, and so on. But they probably hope for very mundane things. That a beloved child finds a job. That a relative's cancer is cured. That the family cat that's been missing for days comes home.

Director: You have cats.

Lawyer: Three of them.

Director: Wouldn't you hope the missing cat would come home?

Lawyer: Of course I would! But I would organize a fantastic search party and find that cat myself.

88

Director: I like how you did that.

Lawyer: Did what?

Director: It was very aristocratic. You enlist the help of others. And then you don't say together we'll find that cat. You say I'll find that cat myself!

Lawyer: Ha, ha. I didn't even notice I did that.

Director: A born aristocrat. Surely you look to the born aristocrats of the past as role models.

Lawyer: Of course I do.

Director: Are these role models somehow above you? The great ones?

Lawyer: They are to be honored and studied. No more, no less. I see them as my peers, cousins, family.

Director: How about the great plebs from the past? Do you admire them? Do you honor them? Do you study them?

Lawyer: I can admire them out of basic human kinship. Do I study them? I have more important things to study and only so much time. Do I honor them? We need to leave that to the plebs.

Director: I thought aristocrats would want to be the source of all honor. Wouldn't that be a useful tool in statecraft?

Lawyer: So, what, are we judges in talent competitions?

Director: You might be. Or you could do what the British crown does and confer honors on those with distinguished careers.

Lawyer: Which do you think is better?

Director: I think your instinct is right.

Lawyer: What's my instinct?

Director: To stay removed.

Lawyer: Tell me why it's right.

Director: The plebs need their own sphere away from you. And you, you need to limit your contact with the plebs.

Lawyer: I know that. But tell me why you think that's so.

Director: Aside from distaste? You need to keep your focus.

Lawyer: Yes! You hit it right on. It is matter of taste, yes. But it's also a matter of expediency. We have to save our energies for our work—not squander them in indulging inferior plebs.

Director: Remind me why the plebs are inferior.

Lawyer: They care most about the lowest things. It's in their nature.

Director: And you care most about the highest things. I seem to recall a thinker who said there is a pyramid of human needs. You satisfy all the lower needs so you can focus on the highest.

Lawyer: It's true. But I'm skeptical of these psychological theories. They assume we all want the same things. What do they call their highest thing? Self-actualization? If I am a full lord of the realm, you'd better believe I'm self-actualized in a way different than they think.

Director: No doubt. Many theorists have a democratic bias. Are these the ones you would censor?

Lawyer: If we tried to censor every professor with a democratic bias, we might as well just close the schools and start from scratch.

Director: But I thought your regime would come about in a turning of the tide. Surely there would be professors sympathetic to your cause.

Lawyer: Plebeian professors looking for favor? I'd rather have aristocrats write the books.

Director: But I thought aristocrats would be writing for other aristocrats.

Lawyer: They would, but maybe those with a taste for writing could pen basic tracts for plebs. But I should tell you. I have doubts about universal literacy.

Director: You liked when Latin was the language of the elite?

Lawyer: I did. Something about that always captured my imagination. Just think, being able to write in an excellent way that is understood only by your peers.

Director: And then there would be a vulgate, like Italian, English, or French. The language of the people.

Lawyer: The vulgar, to call them what they are.

Director: How would an elite language develop?

Lawyer: Well, we can do what those in the Middle Ages did and use a language from the past. I recommend Greek. It's more fluid than Latin. I think you'd like it because it expresses philosophy best.

Director: Best? I don't know about that. Most elegantly, perhaps. But elegance, to a philosopher, can be a matter of aesthetics, not truth. I see this as a danger for aristocrats.

Lawyer: To favor elegance to truth? Our age certainly doesn't make that mistake. There is so little elegance now it's shocking. Everything is so rude and crass.

Director: It's in poor taste.

Lawyer: Exactly.

89

Director: So we're going to have two classes. Will there be subclasses?

Lawyer: There are always sub-classes, classes within classes. But formally? There will be two—the few and the many; aristocrats and plebs.

Director: And there will be equality within each class?

Lawyer: Aristocrats look upon one another as peers; plebs see one another as equals. That's as it should be.

Director: What do you do if there is inequality among the peers?

Lawyer: The peers join together and straighten it out before it becomes a serious problem.

Director: And if there is inequality among the plebs?

Lawyer: We absolutely will not tolerate this.

Director: I'm somewhat surprised. You won't follow the principle of divide and conquer?

Lawyer: Who said anything about conquering the plebs? They belong to us. We want a strong pleb class—one that can support our weight.

Director: The stronger they are the higher you can climb?

Lawyer: Just so.

Director: How does equality make them strong?

Lawyer: It cuts down on jealousies and resentment.

Director: Won't they feel jealousies and resentment toward the few?

Lawyer: At worst I think they'll feel we're a necessary evil.

Director: Aristocracy as the worst form of government except for all the others.

Lawyer: Yes, it often comes down to this. In fact, maybe that's the rule for all regimes. Whatever is least bad wins—until that regime itself turns out to be most bad of all the rest.

Director: What makes an aristocracy bad?

Lawyer: Inequality among the peers. It tends to collapse into monarchy or tyranny, depending.

Director: What makes for inequality?

Lawyer: Concentration of wealth among the very few. To protect themselves from the few, they sometimes choose a one.

Director: A king?

Lawyer: Sure, call it a king. But it can go by other names.

Director: Who would have thought that equality would be the key to aristocracy?

Lawyer: I know, it's somewhat ironic but true.

Director: It's funny, though. I would have thought love would be the key to aristocracy.

Lawyer: I thought we already dispensed with love.

Director: Romantic love, maybe. But what about brotherly love?

Lawyer: Ah. Say more.

Director: Brotherly love makes for unity. Could unity be the key?

Lawyer: You really have a very good point. Unity is the key.

Director: And what about with the plebs? Is unity their key?

Lawyer: I don't know if it's the key. But I do know there can be no unity without equality.

Director: So is it equality for the sake of unity for both the many and the few?

Lawyer: Again, I don't know. Plebs may want equality for the sake of independence.

Director: Aristocrats don't want independence?

Lawyer: An aristocrat doesn't have to want independence. An aristocrat is born with independence.

Director: So plebs have to earn their independence.

Lawyer: Yes. It's not a given for them.

Director: And that's because they lack wealth.

Lawyer: Wealth, which allows for an aristocratic upbringing. Yes.

Director: What if an aristocrat adopted a pleb?

Lawyer: That would be a mistake.

Director: Why?

Lawyer: We've talked about the importance of blood.

Director: Don't you mean the belief in blood?

Lawyer: Certain beliefs are very useful, Director.

Director: No doubt. But useful in what cause?

90

Lawyer: Unity, for one. As the bloodline grows more...

Director: ...pure?

Lawyer: Pure, yes. But I want to say something important here. I don't care if you're black, white, yellow, red, purple, or green. Color has nothing—nothing—to do with purity.

Director: It's all about excellence here.

Lawyer: It really is. Give me the best of every so-called race, and I will give you the aristocracy the world has never seen.

Director: Would you be forming a new race?

Lawyer: You want me to say I'll be forming a master race. Forget about race. These people will simply be the best.

Director: Where does genetic engineering fit into this?

Lawyer: It doesn't. I would ban the practice. There's too much focus on genes.

Director: But you spoke of blood.

Lawyer: I should have spoken of soil, as well. Blood may in large part be genes; but soil is the environment. It's where your roots are set. Blood without soil is next to nothing.

Director: And soil without blood?

Lawyer: A desert.

Director: And if we water the desert with blood?

Lawyer: We get a Joshua tree.

Director: Which is twisted and bristled.

Lawyer: The metaphor has its limits.

Director: Indeed it does. What's the best sort of soil?

Lawyer: Parents who refuse to coddle the child.

Director: Loveless parents refuse to coddle the child.

Lawyer: It's harder, and better, to love and refuse.

Director: And the best among the plebs?

Lawyer: They will love.

Director: And coddle?

Lawyer: They will certainly coddle. And for this they are weak.

Director: I know average people who don't coddle their kids. Why are you so sure they plebs will coddle?

Lawyer: They believe in unconditional love.

Director: What's wrong with that?

Lawyer: What's right with that? Why create an atmosphere in which anything goes?

Director: Aristocrats know better love?

Lawyer: They do. They refuse to love those who refuse to try.

Director: What if they try and fail? Do you love them less?

Lawyer: You'd like to think I'm cold.

Director: I'd like to think you are what you are. What do you love?

Lawyer: My own.

Director: Your own family, friends, peers?

Lawyer: Yes, of course.

Director: But not unconditionally.

Lawyer: That's right. It's probably easiest to explain with my peers. I love them for their love and pursuit of excellence. If they stop loving and pursuing, why should I love them?

Director: Why indeed. Do you think the plebs love the plebs?

Lawyer: I think they do in a similar way.

Director: They don't love each other unconditionally?

Lawyer: Of course they don't. Unconditional love with them is most often reserved for their kids.

91

Director: I'd like to make a general observation.

Lawyer: Please.

Director: The aristocratic regime we're talking about isn't replacing a democracy.

Lawyer: No doubt. It's replacing an oligarchy of the fantastically rich. And it will give people more control over their lives than they have now.

Director: How so?

Lawyer: The oligarchs, or plutocrats, completely control the economy. Let there be no doubt, despite all the pious talk about small businesses. The economy is the primary means of control in our regime. This means the oligarchs control the primary means of control.

Director: How does it differ with the aristocrats?

Lawyer: I know I said we'd have command and control of the economy. But that will only be until it gets itself back up and running. We're not seeking endless wealth. It follows that we're not seeking endless control.

Director: An interesting argument. So there's less control in an aristocracy than a plutocracy.

Lawyer: The truth is we really don't like the plebs. The less we can have to do with them the better. Let them run their own economy.

Director: Do plutocrats like the plebs?

Lawyer: I think they often love the plebs. They see their own success mirrored in the plebs' eyes. I mean, who are they trying to impress? Aristocrats seek to impress their own. But that's only as a secondary thing. Excellence is the key.

Director: Would you say plutocrats love to wow the plebs?

Lawyer: I think that puts it well, yes. An aristocrat couldn't care less what a pleb might think.

Director: But there are exceptions?

Lawyer: There are always exceptions. I'm speaking in general terms.

Director: Why couldn't you care less?

Lawyer: Because their judgment isn't sound. Remember, they are always on the make, always trying to get ahead. That colors the way they think.

Director: Does ambition color the way you think?

Lawyer: You're asking because aristocrats are ambitious.

Director: Well?

Lawyer: Ambition colors the way we think, But the color is good.

Director: Who can argue with that? But does an ambitious pleb have the same color?

Lawyer: They're ambitious for excellence? If so, it might be a related hue. I can grant them that. But these are exceptional people we're talking about. The general color of a pleb's thought is mud.

Director: Tell me your color. Scarlet? Have I guessed?

Lawyer: It's just a metaphor. But scarlet is my favorite hue.

Director: Do you like all shades of red?

Lawyer: Crimson, maroon, you name it—I do. It's the color of blood.

Director: Maybe now I understand why vampires are portrayed as aristocrats.

Lawyer: Ha, ha. Yes, I've noticed. It's because they think we suck the blood out of the plebs.

Director: But you think the plebs will prosper under you.

Lawyer: More so than they do now.

Director: Will you have to gain the support of the people to put you into power?

Lawyer: If we do, it changes the dynamics of our rule.

Director: You'd be beholden to them?

Lawyer: That's what we have to avoid.

Director: But isn't it like finance? A certain amount of debt is good.

Lawyer: If anything, the plebs should feel indebted to us. That makes the taxes go better.

Director: They would owe you for creating a regime that saves them from tyranny?

Lawyer: Yes. If we really save them from that—from mob rule or an actual tyrant—I think the sensible ones, of which there are more than a few, would acknowledge their debt, if only to themselves.

Director: More than a few of the plebs are sensible?

Lawyer: What do they call it? Scared straight? That's what they are.

92

Director: Does it follow that...

Lawyer: Does what follow?

Director: ...that you'd do well to keep the people afraid?

Lawyer: Of us? I'd rather have respect than fear.

Director: Yes, but maybe a little external fear would help.

Lawyer: Oh, that's a trick as old as statesmanship itself. Judicious use of enemies is a given.

Director: Even if they're not really dangerous?

Lawyer: I'm not in favor of that. The only danger I would use is real.

Director: Why do you care to make the distinction?

Lawyer: Because I like to think I'm an honorable man. Besides, if we start manipulating the plebs, where does it all end? No place good, I think.

Director: You're better than most democratic leaders. They manipulate no end. Hmm.

Lawyer: What is it?

Director: I was just struck with an idea. Do you think others of the few would think like you on this matter?

Lawyer: That it's better not to manipulate? Of course. But what are you thinking?

Director: You could just, eventually, take over the federal government and leave all state and local government to the plebs. The structure is already in place. Relatively little manipulation required.

Lawyer: That's an interesting thought. Who knows? Maybe we will. It's not as if a sort of oligarchy hasn't been running the federal government for past few hundred years.

Director: Then from the people's perspective very little will have changed.

Lawyer: Except for the fact that they'll have excellent government this time.

Director: Would the aristocrats be fair?

Lawyer: Scrupulously so. What interest do we have in being unfair? Remember, we are driven by honor.

Director: Plus you have no personal or business entanglements with the plebs.

Lawyer: Exactly. We can afford to be fair.

Director: You're almost convincing me that this is a good idea.

Lawyer: What holds you back?

Director: Will you be fair to your peers?

Lawyer: Why wouldn't we?

Director: Jealousies.

Lawyer: Ah, that old monster again.

Director: Be honest with me. Is sexual jealousy the Achilles' heel?

Lawyer: It probably is.

Director: Is there a need for clear sexual morals to prevent the worst?

Lawyer: What, make adultery a capital crime? No, thanks. We'll just have to do our best.

Director: Who is stricter in sexual morals? Aristocrats or plebs?

Lawyer: I don't know. The plebs, I suppose.

Director: Why do you think they are?

Lawyer: Their families don't have the support and protection ours have. They need their morals. We don't. And if you don't believe me, I'll tell you this. Aristocrats really don't know much divorce.

Director: Because there's more than love in the marriage?

Lawyer: Yes, marriage is a true institution for us.

Director: The aristocratic family is the bedrock of the regime.

Lawyer: Democrats won't believe it, but family is more important here.

Director: So how do you punish adultery?

Lawyer: Through social sanctions.

Director: That really cuts to the quick?

Lawyer: Society is the air an aristocrat breathes.

Director: How do plebs punish adultery?

Lawyer: Through expensive divorce. And pain when children are involved.

Director: Don't they also have social sanctions?

Lawyer: Oh, of course they do. But their society can't compare to ours.

Director: Your society is more intense?

Lawyer: Look at it this way. If you're philandering pleb from Boston, and you come under pressure, you can up and move to San Francisco—and no one will care. You can start anew. But aristocrats get no fresh start. There is no re-inventing yourself when you're one of the few. You were invented before you were born.

Director: That's an excellent point. You're sort of trapped.

Lawyer: Yes. It isn't all milk and honey for an aristocrat.

Director: You operate under strict expectations.

Lawyer: We do. But this is also good. The only way out is up. Excellence.

Director: I never looked at it that way before. But can you ever go high enough to be free?

Lawyer: I honestly don't know. I've gone high by most standards. But I wouldn't say I'm free.

Director: Maybe you lack the right environment.

Lawyer: I've often wondered about that.

Director: Could this wonder be what makes you long for aristocracy?

Lawyer: Who can say for sure? What about you? Do you feel free?

Director: At times I do. But often not.

Lawyer: What makes for the difference?

Director: Who I'm talking to. The company I keep.

Lawyer: That's the thing with aristocracy. It's either very good, or terribly bad— the company, that is.

Director: I'm sure there is no greater difference than that between an aristocracy in its prime, and one in decay.

Lawyer: You're right about that. And I don't kid myself. Nothing lasts forever.

Director: No, it's true. But do you think an aristocracy can be in its prime right from the start?

Lawyer: It's very unlikely. There's lots of turbulence at the start.

Director: Then why do people look to founders as the exceptional class?

Lawyer: Because to overcome the turbulence takes virtue of the first rank.

Director: So it's not that these people are unhappy—it's that their virtuous?

Lawyer: Yes. That's why they deserve their fame.

Director: And what of those in the golden age of the regime?

Lawyer: We admire their satisfaction with their lot.

Director: I thought you'd say we admire their excellence.

Lawyer: But that, Director, is precisely their lot.

93

Director: The lot is what allows for the excellence.

Lawyer: Of course. Aristocrats are practical realists. Yes, the excellence comes from one's own effort; yes, the excellence cannot be without material support.

Director: How do you explain the poor who at times develop great talents?

Lawyer: Great talent does not necessarily mean an excellent life.

Director: What goes into an excellent life?

Lawyer: A sense of duty, responsibility, persuasiveness, courage, an open mind, and exceptional skill in rule.

Director: The traits you listed all go into rule, don't they?

Lawyer: Yes, but rule is a very broad topic. It encompasses knowledge of men.

Director: All this while when you've been speaking of rule you were thinking of knowledge of men?

Lawyer: Of course. Weren't you?

Director: Knowledge of men is the grandest topic there is. What else is worth knowing? How do you gain this knowledge?

Lawyer: We're trained in the ways of men from early youth on up.

Director: Does the training grow in sophistication as the youths grow in age?

Lawyer: Naturally. But we learn the rudiments at an early age.

Director: How does this compare with the plebs?

Lawyer: There is no comparison. They from an early age have their heads filled with nonsense. So many types of nonsense it would be hard to explain.

Director: What is nonsense number one?

Lawyer: All you need is love. It simply isn't true—not if you want to live a full life.

Director: You need an inheritance.

Lawyer: Yes. You need to be grounded. A life income does that for you.

Director: I suppose nothing grounds like money in the bank from earliest youth on up.

Lawyer: Yes. And don't tell me you know grounded plebs. So do I. But they are the exception—and they're not always happy.

Director: But are they satisfied?

Lawyer: It's hard to be satisfied with their lot. But there are some exceptional cases here and there.

Director: You'd promote them to lieutenant or whatever.

Lawyer: Yes, I would. It would be an honor for them

Director: Would you treat them as equals?

Lawyer: Not social equals, no. But maybe as human equals.

Director: I think we're found the chink in your armor.

Lawyer: How so?

Director: You admit there is something higher than the aristocracy.

Lawyer: You're mistaken. The merely human is lower than the aristocratic.

Director: Is it something like saying we have a certain animal nature in common?

Lawyer: Yes, something like that.

Director: So it goes animal, human, aristocratic.

Lawyer: Yes, you put it well.

Director: How about this? Animal, human, plebeian, aristocratic.

Lawyer: Hmm. I'll have to think about that.

Director: Is the question whether being a pleb in your regime debases or elevates man?

Lawyer: That is the question. I suppose good aristocratic rule should elevate the plebs.

Director: What if they don't want to be elevated?

Lawyer: Well, we can't force them, can we? You can lead a horse to water...

Director: ...but you can't make him drink. But the plebs aren't horses. And I think they're thirsty.

Lawyer: They thirst for excellence?

Director: Some of them do.

Lawyer: These are the ones we'll honor.

Director: What if they don't want the honor?

Lawyer: In theory, it's easy to resent honors given from another class. In practice, they're very hard to refuse.

Director: Especially when accompanied by money?

Lawyer: Especially so. We aristocrats know enough not to give empty honors. We appreciate the value of money. The plebs we favor do, too.

Director: Will they be resented by their peers?

Lawyer: The ones who resent will be on our list.

Director: List?

Lawyer: Of trouble makers.

Director: So you will spy on them.

Lawyer: Of course we will!

Director: What will you do with the troublemakers?

Lawyer: If they're trouble enough we'll banish them. Didn't we talk about this before?

Director: No matter if we did. Let's talk about it now.

Lawyer: What's to say? We must act against subversives.

Director: If they merely resent the ones you favor?

Lawyer: If it's jealousy, that's okay. We know about jealousy. But resentment is a different thing.

Director: How so?

Lawyer: The jealous want what the other has got. The resentful despise what the other has got.

Director: And what they've got came from you.

Lawyer: Yes. And if they despise what we give, they despise what we are.

Director: It doesn't do to despise the few.

Lawyer: It really doesn't.

Director: So you banish them. What of their family and friends?

Lawyer: The friends may already be on our list. And the family might be relieved.

Director: And if they're not?

Lawyer: Then fear will help them hold their tongues.

94

Director: This is the terror you spoke of.

Lawyer: It is.

Director: The fear of being expelled. Where will you send them? To some penal colony?

Lawyer: That really isn't a bad idea. We should establish one somewhere. Maybe up in Alaska?

Director: Don't ask me. I'm not properly equipped to weigh in on these things.

Lawyer: Modesty doesn't become you, if that's what that was.

Director: Maybe life in Alaska would be nice?

Lawyer: With no money and no modern economy to support them?

Director: You'd cut them off from contact with your realm.

Lawyer: Absolutely. No access to our internet and so on. They'll have no contact with our plebs.

Director: But there will be contact with you?

Lawyer: We'll keep an eye on them, and let them know we do.

Director: What if they try to organize resistance from afar?

Lawyer: You've heard of the long arm of the law? Well, the reach of the law-free aristocrat is greater—and more terrible.

Director: Terrible, terror, yes. I suppose each regime has its terror.

Lawyer: Democrats like to deny their terror. But it's there. It has always been there. So don't let them get righteous on you.

Director: I try not to let anyone get righteous on me.

Lawyer: So do I. What do they say? The meek shall inherit the Earth? Well, the righteous are the ones who claim it—and they often win.

Director: The meek aren't righteous?

Lawyer: The righteous pretend to be meek. The truly meek have no truck with righteousness.

Director: Do you have a sympathy for the meek?

Lawyer: You know, I do. They're honest in their meekness. And honesty is a start.

Director: A start toward what?

Lawyer: The limited excellence the plebs can hope to achieve.

Director: Aristocrats are never meek.

Lawyer: Only the deficient among them are.

Director: But don't you want to inherit the Earth?

Lawyer: We want to inherit our inheritance—no more, no less.

Director: Global dominion isn't your thing?

Lawyer: You raise an interesting question. Can there be a global aristocracy?

Director: And a global plebs?

Lawyer: Yes, that's the question. Sad but true, an aristocracy takes some of its shape from its plebs. A global aristocracy assumes a certain oneness of man at the level of the plebs. I'm not sure that's desirable.

Director: Why not?

Lawyer: Diversity.

Director: Aristocrats are in favor of diversity?

Lawyer: No doubt. We need a healthy world. What if we make all the world one? What if all the plebs are the same? And what if we're wrong? What a colossal mess!

Director: You never cease to amaze me, Lawyer. Just when I think I understand your aristocracy you say something like this.

Lawyer: Aristocrats must operate in a limited sphere. This has always been clear. We need something we can control.

Director: Is it a sort of experiment?

Lawyer: The way that democracy is an experiment? That always made me laugh. This republic was as sure of itself and its success as any regime ever was. Yes, the beginning was touch and go. And it took the great second war to really feel the power in your bones. But was it ever really in doubt?

Director: I think it was.

Lawyer: Oh, maybe I'm getting carried away.

Director: Yes, I think you are. I still want to know. Do you think of your aristocracy as an experiment?

Lawyer: I suppose any new regime is an experiment. It depends on our knowledge of men.

Director: And living up to your idea of excellence.

95

Lawyer: Do you really think excellence is just an idea?

Director: It's a way of life in accordance with an idea. How's that?

Lawyer: Fine. We make the idea real in flesh and blood.

Director: Who do you think came up with the idea?

Lawyer: I think it's an idea as old as man himself.

Director: How did it come about?

Lawyer: I don't know, exactly. I suppose people wanted something more.

Director: They had a dream?

Lawyer: Yes, I think they had a dream. And there were a proud few who decided to live up to the dream.

Director: The first aristocrats. The best. Those given to excellence.

Lawyer: Right.

Director: And by virtue of there being aristocrats, there suddenly was a plebs.

Lawyer: I'm not sure.

Director: Why not?

Lawyer: Plebs have a symbiotic relationship with aristocrats. Both benefit from the relationship. Not everyone is fit to be a pleb.

Director: This is very interesting, Lawyer. The plebs are proud of their status?

Lawyer: Yes, when the circumstances are right.

Director: What makes them right?

Lawyer: It happens when the plebs freely acknowledge the virtue of the aristocrats.

Director: And the aristocrats freely acknowledge the virtue of the plebs?

Lawyer: Yes, but there's a difficulty here.

Director: Let me guess. It takes a special sort of person to say, 'I am not equal to you. You are my better.'

Lawyer: And an aristocrat has to be willing to say, 'It's true.'

Director: If only to himself.

Lawyer: Yes.

Director: So in the ideal aristocracy the plebs are willingly plebs.

Lawyer: That's right. And this speaks highly of them. They are friends with truth. They acknowledge the truth. Not so easily done.

Director: Indeed. But how do you know they're not mistaken? How do you know they're telling the truth?

Lawyer: If aristocrats are good at anything, they're good at taking the measure of men.

Director: And if a generation from now you find an aristocrat who's lacking?

Lawyer: This, of course, is the flaw in hereditary right. We find a lesser place for him—and hope blood in the next generation will tell.

Director: Will tell that the line is still strong.

Lawyer: Yes, virtue sometimes skips a generation.

Director: How many generations before you extinguish the rights of the line?

Lawyer: Three.

Director: And then what? Banishment?

Lawyer: No, it's through no fault of their own. We relocate them to another land.

Director: Not to the penal colony.

Lawyer: No, of course not. Just some other decent land that will take them in.

Director: How will they support themselves?

Lawyer: We'll give the a small life pension. Enough to get by. But their kids will have to work.

Director: Won't they suffer from terrible shame?

Lawyer: What can I say? We were forced to this end.

Director: Can't have weak aristocrats ruining the few.

Lawyer: No, the few aren't the few unless can keep themselves clean.

Director: You mean pure.

Lawyer: I do.

Director: Living up to the idea isn't some intellectual exercise.

Lawyer: Of course it isn't. There's nothing intellectual about it.

Director: And that's my fear.

Lawyer: Oh, don't start with that. You know we highly value the life of the mind.

Director: As a little tonic at night before you fall asleep. Your life centers on rule.

Lawyer: It does. And the life of the mind improves our ability to rule.

Director: So you'll only read political philosophers.

Lawyer: Naturally. Though we understand that supposedly apolitical philosophers do have something important to say.

Director: What do they say?

Lawyer: Let's look at metaphysics. Certain metaphysical assumptions can support or undermine a regime.

Director: Is it the same with aesthetics?

Lawyer: No doubt. But once you grasp the implications you no longer need to concern yourself with these philosophers.

Director: So you give your serious time to the descendants of Socrates.

Lawyer: He was the first political philosopher. And it may be true that Plato prettied him up. But that's the line of philosophy that I follow.

Director: Philosophers should be trusted advisors to the few.

Lawyer: Yes. That's their proper role. Like Machiavelli advising Florence's elite.

Director: They tortured Machiavelli as a suspected conspirator against the Medici regime.

Lawyer: That was a mistake. He wasn't part of a conspiracy against the government.

Director: How do you know?

Lawyer: Philosophers don't like to get their hands dirty.

Director: Maybe this one did. Or maybe he was no philosopher.

Lawyer: Why don't you want to believe in his innocence?

Director: Because I've read what he wrote.

96

Lawyer: I intend to write someday.

Director: Why not now?

Lawyer: I don't yet have the experience I'll need.

Director: Experience with an aristocracy.

Lawyer: Yes, even if it's just inching our way closer. That's valuable experience to have and to communicate.

Director: To future peers.

Lawyer: Yes. We have to help our descendants as much as we can.

Director: And even if you're wrong about some things, that can be useful, too.

Lawyer: They can learn from our mistakes.

Director: How can you make sure your work is valuable to future aristocrats?

Lawyer: I have to be totally honest. There can be no little lies.

Director: Why not? Won't they see through them?

Lawyer: Maybe not. Why take the chance?

Director: Agreed. So your book will be about rule?

Lawyer: It will be about life as an aristocrat—regardless of whether I live in an aristocracy or not.

Director: The born aristocrat.

Lawyer: Yes. And the biggest challenge for us at the beginning is gathering up all the natural born aristocrats and confirming them in the cause.

Director: You mean finding ways to ensure they have money.

Lawyer: True. They need means.

Director: And positions of influence?

Lawyer: No doubt.

Director: This sounds like it could be a multi-generational affair.

Lawyer: I've resigned myself to that. Yes, it's possible things will happen more quickly. But I don't like tumult. A gradual change would be better.

Director: So what of the talk of war?

Lawyer: War might be necessary.

Director: Civil war?

Lawyer: That, too.

Director: Sometimes civil wars break out after the war with the foreigners. Why do you think that is?

Lawyer: The foreign war creates a new reality within. Some can't stand this reality and want to bring things back to the way they were.

Director: So again we find the aristocrats opposed to conservatives.

Lawyer: Not quite. We want to preserve—conserve—the new order. Our enemies are dreamers of a time already gone.

Director: So it's realists versus dreamers.

Lawyer: And who do you think will win?

Director: I suppose it depends on who has more force. What happens if the dreamers win?

Lawyer: A nightmare reign follows.

Director: Why is it a nightmare?

Lawyer: Because nothing is worse than when a leader can't see the truth.

Director: Is it like this? You need a shoe to walk in. You wear a size twelve. The leader in charge of shoes figure you have two feet, and six and six make twelve—so he gives you two sixes. You go barefoot the rest of the way.

Lawyer: Something like that, sure. And imagine this happening for all sorts of things.

Director: I can imagine.

Lawyer: It's especially hard on youth.

Director: I don't think it's too easy on the old. Why especially youth?

Lawyer: Youth grow disillusioned from this sort of rule.

Director: You want the youth to have illusions?

Lawyer: Maybe I should say they lose their hope.

Director: I didn't know you wanted your realist aristocrats to be hopeful.

Lawyer: We have rational hopes. When the youths see the irrationality of their leaders, something within them changes.

Director: This change sounds important. What is it, exactly?

Lawyer: They lose their focus on reason and long for revenge.

Director: For having to walk barefoot, so to speak.

Lawyer: Precisely. Revenge is a heady brew. You can ruin your life with revenge.

Director: You and I have both had to wear wrong fitting shoes now and then. How are we not consumed with a desire for revenge?

Lawyer: I focus on my hope for the future. You have philosophy.

Director: You think philosophers can't long for revenge?

Lawyer: Can they?

Director: Philosophers lack the hope for the future you have.

Lawyer: What do they have?

Director: An inordinate desire to improve the present through words.

Lawyer: Conversation.

Director: Yes.

Lawyer: But you put your money where your mouth is. I've seen you do it.

Director: But my preference is words.

Lawyer: You love words.

Director: I love flesh and blood people—and the words they speak.

Lawyer: We could really use you for the cause.

Director: Philosophy is my cause. But who knows? Our paths may intersect for a while.

Lawyer: Philosophy can only be secondary thing for us. Young aristocrats must learn first and foremost the importance of deeds.

Director: I'm aware of the importance of deeds—the primary importance, even. But there are those who want to use words to give the deed meaning.

Lawyer: The deed should speak for itself.

Director: I agree. I would tear down their words until the naked truth remains.

Lawyer: I want our youths to always get the naked truth. It will make them strong and wise.

Director: But I suppose if people heard us they'd think we're talking about terrible deeds.

Lawyer: There will be terrible deeds. But there will also be deeds of love and compassion.

Director: The full range of things human?

Lawyer: The very full range.

97

Director: Is the full range possible in a democracy?

Lawyer: It is not.

Director: Why not?

Lawyer: The top of the pyramid is chopped off.

Director: What about the super rich?

Lawyer: Most of the super rich are simply very wealthy plebs.

Director: They lack elevated sentiment.

Lawyer: Yes. They are not refined, though they often buy refined things.

Director: Does refinement come from learning the naked truth from youth on up?

Lawyer: Some of the super rich are super rich precisely because they were exposed to naked truth from youth on up.

Director: But there is exposure and there is exposure?

Lawyer: Absolutely. We expose our youths and then we advise. Also, we don't over-expose. A little exposure to certain things goes a very long way.

Director: Are the plebs over-exposed?

Lawyer: Not if we can help it.

Director: Would you try to refine the plebs?

Lawyer: To the extent that's possible, yes. A rising tide lifts all ships.

Director: So what will you do, have cultural events for them?

Lawyer: Yes. Concerts, plays, exhibits—anything that might help.

Director: But when speaking of over-exposure, you weren't speaking of cultural things.

Lawyer: While I do believe you can saturate yourself in culture—to your detriment—I was speaking of other things, terrible things.

Director: We must not shelter our youths.

Lawyer: Not completely, at least—no.

Director: Can we shelter the plebs?

Lawyer: Like our children? I don't know. I suppose it makes sense.

Director: Censorship once again?

Lawyer: Yes. We give them the truth but limit how much they see.

Director: Are you talking about pure repetition?

Lawyer: The news today goes on and on and beats a thing to death, inflaming spirits as it does. I would have them state the truth once and leave it at that.

Director: So those who want to know can know; and those who don't pay attention miss out.

Lawyer: That's the way it should be. Freedom of information and lack of mindless repetition.

Director: What about analysis of the facts of the news?

Lawyer: None.

Director: But only for the plebs?

Lawyer: The few will get analysis in the debates that go into rule.

Director: Ah. I didn't know you were debating all day.

Lawyer: How else do you think peers proceed? Remember, we're equals.

Director: Could a pleb ever see one of these debates?

Lawyer: They won't be televised, if that's what you mean.

Director: What about the elevated plebs, your lieutenants and such?

Lawyer: Certain of them will have access, of course. When we trust, we trust.

Director: Why not televise the debates?

Lawyer: Because we need to present a unified front.

Director: The few are one. There is no weakness of disunity here.

Lawyer: Precisely. Why confuse the plebs or give them reason to think they might exploit our weaknesses?

Director: And overthrow the regime.

Lawyer: To put it bluntly, yes.

Director: How about releasing a transcript? Who would read that?

Lawyer: Two kinds of people. One, those who long for elevation. Two, those who long to overthrow.

Director: What makes the difference between the two?

Lawyer: It's very hard to say. Both probably have equal ability.

Director: Do you admit as much?

Lawyer: Yes, of course. Strong regimes necessarily have strong enemies. Ours is no exception.

Director: What do you do with the strong enemies?

Lawyer: It depends what they do.

Director: What if they talk subversive talk?

Lawyer: It's to the penal colony with them.

Director: For just talking some talk?

Lawyer: The habit of speaking against the government breeds deeper crimes.

Director: So you nip it in the bud. No freedom of speech.

Lawyer: The ultimate location of free speech is in the debates of the few.

Director: Even the few must watch what they say outside these debates?

Lawyer: We all must watch what we say—wherever we say it.

98

Director: Why must the few watch what they say?

Lawyer: It's healthy to have a place for speech. Beyond that is indulgence.

Director: Will the youth be allowed to hear the debates?

Lawyer: No, only fully fledged peers.

Director: So the peers must keep secrets from their families.

Lawyer: They can tell them the truth but spare the details.

Director: Why confuse them, right?

Lawyer: Why confuse them, yes.

Director: So it's only the head of the household who can handle the truth in all its detail.

Lawyer: Do you think that's bad?

Director: I don't know. I usually argue in favor of truth being spread. What's wrong with truth?

Lawyer: Truth is complex. Policy is not.

Director: Policies must be simple and clear.

Lawyer: Think of it like an athletic event. The athlete trains for grueling years. Then there's the event, where he is graceful, proud, and strong. Simple.

Director: He wins or he doesn't. The policy is successful or not. Do you let failure be known, or do you cover it up?

Lawyer: We let it be known. Why hide the obvious? We go back and try again.

Director: What happens to the architects of the policy?

Lawyer: Their words carry that much less force in debate.

Director: Do the young carry that much more force than the old?

Lawyer: The old have wisdom; the young have vim. Both persuade in their own way.

Director: I see why wisdom might persuade. Why might vim?

Lawyer: Things seem possible to youth that seem impossible to age. Sometimes the young persuade the middle and carry the day.

Director: What's something that's impossible for an aristocracy?

Lawyer: Pity for the plebs.

Director: Why that?

Lawyer: It's the ultimate mark of decay. Aristocrats must stand firm on their ground. Their ground is the plebs.

Director: The plebs must be firm.

Lawyer: Firm, yes. Their virtue in this regime is to be solid ground.

Director: How do you ensure this ground?

Lawyer: We've already said. A strong economy, censorship, fear, hope for some to rise.

Director: And let's not forget safety.

Lawyer: Yes, that, too—of course. Safety is a paramount thing.

Director: Safety alone is enough for some.

Lawyer: Those aren't the ones we want. They would be happy under a tyrant who keeps the peace.

Director: How do you differ from a tyrant?

Lawyer: A tyrant is crass. We are refined.

Director: That's it? That's the only difference?

Lawyer: Everything follows from this. A tyrant is crass in his judgments. We are refined in ours.

Director: Can there be justice in the crass?

Lawyer: A rough kind of justice, sure. But that only satisfies the lowest common denominator.

Director: Is there such a thing as the highest common denominator?

Lawyer: There certainly is. And we want to make it higher and higher still.

Director: Toward what end?

Lawyer: It's a game, really.

Director: Life is a game?

Lawyer: To see how high we can climb.

Director: One alone?

Lawyer: Yes and no. Yes, the highest high will likely be achieved by one or very few. No, the grounds of support must rise to allow the highest climb.

Director: Like a sort of base camp on a mountain?

Lawyer: Sure, something like that.

Director: A rising tide....

Lawyer: That's exactly right.

Director: What makes the tide rise?

Lawyer: Prosperity. And I don't mean simple economic prosperity.

Director: You mean living a good life, noble or pleb.

Lawyer: Well, just pleb, actually. Nobles will live more than a good life. Excellence, remember.

Director: But prosperity for the plebs means living a good life.

Lawyer: Yes, a good life. That's our promise to them.

Director: Promise? This is the first I'm hearing of a promise. Is it some sort of social contract?

Lawyer: No, not some base contract. But a promise implied by our noble hearts.

99

Director: What's wrong with contracts?

Lawyer: Contracts come from the world of petty business interests. Government should ennoble.

Director: Government should lift us up, not press us down.

Lawyer: We don't press down the plebs, you know. And we do lift them up.

Director: Yes, you make sure they're like dirt piled high that you then pack down until firm. Then there's no pressing down.

Lawyer: Fair enough. But we'll have no contract with them.

Director: What will you have?

Lawyer: An understanding.

Director: Based on what? Fear?

Lawyer: Mutual advantage.

Director: Sounds like a contract to me.

Lawyer: If you can't tell the difference between a contract and an understanding, I can't help you.

Director: What happens when a contract is violated?

Lawyer: There is base legal recourse.

Director: And when an understanding is violated?

Lawyer: Honor is lost.

Director: Which is much more serious than legal proceedings.

Lawyer: Infinitely so.

Director: Infinity can't be measured.

Lawyer: Infinity marks a difference of type, not of degree.

Director: Infinity separates the many from the few.

Lawyer: Yes, as it separates the philosophers from the unthinking.

Director: I think the unthinking think at times, just not all of the time.

Lawyer: And philosophers think all the time.

Director: Well, I'm not entirely sure.

Lawyer: How so?

Director: Thinking can lead us to an act; but when it comes time to act, we might not think.

Lawyer: I think that's very true. When we peers deliberate, we think. But once we've decided on what to do, we act—no thought involved.

Director: Yes, but what if between deliberating and doing new information comes to light?

Lawyer: We must stop and rethink.

Director: And if afterwards you change your mind?

Lawyer: We must deliberate again.

Director: And if you must deliberate again and again?

Lawyer: We must be fools.

Director: Why? The foolish thing would be to act without deliberating again.

Lawyer: Yes, but you've heard of analysis paralysis?

Director: I have.

Lawyer: The few can ill afford that.

Director: Do you think that's what philosophers do?

Lawyer: Do I think they're paralyzed? Or do I think they paralyze others?

Director: Either.

Lawyer: They don't seem paralyzed to me. I look to you. You've always acted when you must. And you couldn't have served our country in war without doing that.

Director: But do I paralyze others? And when might that be good?

Lawyer: I suppose if there were a subversive pleb who talked philosophy with you and grew perplexed, so he didn't act out his subversion—that would be good.

Director: And an aristocrat?

Lawyer: The same.

Director: There are subversive aristocrats?

Lawyer: More than I care to admit.

Director: What do they do?

Lawyer: They pity the plebs. They fail to acknowledge excellence.

Director: How could they fail to acknowledge excellence?

Lawyer: They think it's nothing more than sublimated cruelty.

Director: Is it?

Lawyer: I don't know. Let's say it is. So what? It's excellence nonetheless.

Director: Yes, but are you in favor of cruelty?

Lawyer: I'm in favor of cruelty against the self.

Director: What does that mean?

Lawyer: You lash yourself mercilessly on.

Director: If you treat yourself that way, how will you treat others?

Lawyer: We can expect much of ourselves and very little of others.

Director: And when we do? Contempt?

Lawyer: Not necessarily. If the others live up to their abilities, no contempt.

Director: But if they don't?

Lawyer: Then they are worthy of contempt.

Director: Contempt is all about failure to be what you are?

Lawyer: That puts it well. We all must be what we are.

100

Director: What's wrong with an underachiever?

Lawyer: In a pleb? He's beneath our contempt. In an aristocrat? He harms the cause.

Director: How?

Lawyer: You wonder why we can't just let him be? It's the example he sets to the young.

Director: It's cool to be slack.

Lawyer: Right. And we must show everyone it's not cool.

Director: So let me see if I understand. A person might be performing in the ninetieth percentile but still be slacking?

Lawyer: Those with great natural gifts are the worst.

Director: Why?

Lawyer: They're seductive to the rest.

Director: Those with abilities not as great.

Lawyer: Yes. But with their equals—

Director: —I thought they all were equals.

Lawyer: Some are more equal than others. Their equals will have contempt for them.

Director: Because they see them as less than cool.

Lawyer: Whatever the reason, it is so.

Director: So what do you do? Banish the underachiever?

Lawyer: We take away his honors and reveal him for what he is.

Director: Which is?

Lawyer: You always need it all spelled out. A slacker.

Director: Slacker must have a special meaning in circles of excellence.

Lawyer: In a culture given to striving, to slack is the greatest sin.

Director: You make me think of the pleb and super rich economy when it's at full tilt. To slack is the ultimate sin. Who is it that commits the ultimate sin?

Lawyer: I don't know what you're asking.

Director: Those who listen to the Devil.

Lawyer: Well, yes. The Devil causes slack.

Director: And yet they say idleness plays into the Devil's intrigue. Idleness and leisure are closely linked.

Lawyer: That's why we have an ambitious leisure.

Director: Is it really leisure if it's ambitious?

Lawyer: Shouldn't leisure be free? Is that what you're asking?

Director: I am.

Lawyer: No. Freedom is the most overrated thing in the world.

Director: Overrated and underutilized

Lawyer: Yes. Freedom should be utilized, not squandered.

Director: Idleness, slack wastes freedom.

Lawyer: Of course it does.

Director: So freedom isn't free.

Lawyer: Oh, you know freedom is free.

Director: But if there is no choice but to excel....

Lawyer: Look, aristocrats only want what's best. So if you want to slack, just hope you're one of the plebs.

Director: But if you have the misfortune of being born into an aristocracy?

Lawyer: Then you must try for all you're worth.

Director: It doesn't seem fair.

Lawyer: No, I know. The poor plebs don't have the proper incentive to try.

Director: I meant we shouldn't be forced to try.

Lawyer: Why not? Once you really try, you never go back.

Director: Why is that, if it's true?

Lawyer: There's no satisfaction like that which comes from making our greatest effort.

Director: We give all we've got and what we get in return is great?

Lawyer: Yes, exactly so.

Director: What if we give our all, succeed, and don't like what we see?

Lawyer: Why wouldn't we like it?

Director: It comes at a cost we don't like to pay.

Lawyer: What cost?

Director: Our freedom. Freedom to do nothing, but freedom nonetheless.

Lawyer: You don't want to be in harness all the time.

Director: No, I don't. I guess I'll never be a proper aristocrat.

Lawyer: No one ever said you would.

Director: Can you say more?

Lawyer: You're a philosopher, not an aristocrat. What more needs to be said?

Director: What is it about philosophy that distances it from aristocracy?

Lawyer: Oh, I don't know how to explain. Aristocrats want to know enough to do. Philosophers want to do enough to know.

Director: That's a neat little saying. It's probably true.

101

Lawyer: You don't take offense?

Director: Why would I? Did you intend it as a slight?

Lawyer: No, just as the truth. It's a question of values.

Director: And you think I value knowledge more than action.

Lawyer: Don't you?

Director: It depends on the action. Some actions are very knowledge dependent. In those cases, I value knowledge for the sake of action.

Lawyer: For the sake of the knowledge to be gained by the action.

Director: So what if it's true? The action is the same. Why not learn from it?

Lawyer: Okay, you have a point. But I can say, in turn, the knowledge you gain is for the sake of further, greater action.

Director: Yes, we can go on and on—and we still don't know the difference between an aristocrat and a philosopher.

Lawyer: Philosophers don't want to rule.

Director: Why not?

Lawyer: Rule is taxing. The energy could be spent on dialogue.

Director: At the end of a long day at work, I've been known to refresh myself in conversation with friends.

Lawyer: Alright. You tell me why philosophers don't want to rule.

Director: It depends on the philosopher. Some want to rule; many don't.

Lawyer: Why is it only some?

Director: Their circumstances led them that way.

Lawyer: Through no fault of their own.

Director: Oh, I know what you're trying to say. Philosophers don't look down on rule. They would just rather not take part.

Lawyer: It's beneath them.

Director: No, I'd rather say it's above them. Over their heads.

Lawyer: Above as in better, or above as in social sphere.

Director: I see you're stuck on this. Above as in a social sphere.

Lawyer: But don't philosophers move in the highest circles?

Director: They can and sometimes do.

Lawyer: Then why won't they rule?

Director: It interferes with philosophy.

Lawyer: It takes up all your time?

Director: Yes. But that's not what I had in mind.

Lawyer: Then tell me what's on your mind.

Director: Take one thing. Censorship. Philosophers angle for complete freedom of speech. Does that make us enemies of the state?

Lawyer: You can't entertain subversives. You know that.

Director: But what if we can learn something from them?

Lawyer: What could you possibly learn?

Director: For one, they might be acutely aware of some of the failings of the state.

Lawyer: So it's philosophy for the sake of the state?

Director: No. I'm just citing a byproduct that might be helpful to you.

Lawyer: And what would be helpful to you?

Director: A fresh perspective.

Lawyer: Do you really crave the new?

Director: I don't crave the new. But I also don't turn it away on principle. Admit it. Once your regime is established, there is no state more conservative minded than an aristocracy.

Lawyer: We have the most to lose.

Director: Income for life and beyond, a life of leisure spent on rule—a lot to lose.

Lawyer: And still, that's not enough for you?

Director: I don't want to spend my life in rule.

Lawyer: I guess I'll never understand.

Director: Rule takes a certain posture of soul. Do you agree?

Lawyer: I do.

Director: And you must always maintain this posture.

Lawyer: True.

Director: Well, when engaged in philosophy one must be willing to bend.

Lawyer: You're saying we're not flexible.

Director: Yes. No doubt you have some flexibility when dealing with one another. But on a philosophical scale? You barely bend at all.

Lawyer: And what does this looseness get you? Truth?

Director: At times. It's all about access to truth.

Lawyer: But I know philosophers have said sometimes you see truth best from above.

Director: It's true. And sometimes you aristocrats will see the truth. But sometimes you need to go beneath.

Lawyer: Are you talking morally?

Director: No. I'm talking about position in life. To really understand the plebs you need the view from above, at level, and beneath.

Director: And to understand the aristocracy?

Director: Who can truly understand that aristocracy? There is no going above.

Lawyer: Ha! I'm softening to your thought.

Director: Give me a position above the aristocracy and I might take it—for a while.

Lawyer: Well, I would never take a position beneath the plebs. So you're going to have to help me here.

Director: You want a sort of spy?

Lawyer: I do. And it pays very well.

Director: I'll have to think it over. But for now there are no plebs, only people.

Lawyer: And no aristocrats, only me.

Director: And a handful of your friends.

Lawyer: You have no idea how secretive we must be.

Director: I can imagine. There is little more despised in a democracy than an aristocrat within.

Lawyer: Thanks for the reminder.

102

Director: But there is nothing quite so romantic as an aristocrat.

Lawyer: Yes, in romances about the past.

Director: There can be romances in the present.

Lawyer: Aristocracy is forbidden.

Director: Which makes it all the more enticing.

Lawyer: Seductive, you mean.

Director: Sure, seductive. How would you like to be a great seducer?

Lawyer: I have a wife and kid.

Director: Oh, you know what I mean. But let's say persuade rather than seduce. You could persuade the many to accept the few.

Lawyer: Prepare them for when the time comes? I'd like to do that. But how? Do I go on television and preach the faith?

Director: Do what you do with your friends and widen the circle a bit.

Lawyer: Look for sympathizers? But you know the problem. Everyone I talk to will think I'm recruiting them, the less than excellent them, to be aristocrats, too.

Director: Hmm. I see what you mean. I don't see a way around it. So maybe all you can do is prepare your friends.

Lawyer: And then when the time comes we pull back the curtain and—hope they'll like what they see?

Director: Yes.

Lawyer: You're either setting us up for a fall or placing very great faith in us.

Director: Neither. I just don't see another way.

Lawyer: Maybe the trick is scrapping the romance. Maybe we find those who can write histories that show all the good that came of aristocracies in the past.

Director: There's an idea. Academics can sometimes have more freedom than the popular press.

Lawyer: The academic works will reach the attention of the few. And the popularizers can help prepare the many.

Director: And they're prepared if they see aristocracy isn't so bad.

Lawyer: Yes. But they'll never be enthusiastic about aristocracy, not unless their life hangs in the balance.

Director: You're right. The many, unless compelled, rarely love the few. This is just simple knowledge of men.

Lawyer: I agree. It's one thing to admire our betters. It's another thing to love.

Director: It must take a lot for the few to gain the admiration of the many.

Lawyer: It takes a very great deal. There must be the utmost probity in all our dealings with them. They might envy, but we must avoid giving them reasons to hate.

Director: But would a prosperous pleb envy the few?

Lawyer: Why wouldn't he?

Director: He knows he's not cut from the cloth to do what you do.

Lawyer: Not everyone wants to live up to the highest standards, true.

Director: And maybe that's how it should be. The plebs will look on in wonder and obey, if your commands are mostly for good they can see.

Lawyer: I don't mind being wondered at, at all. In fact, it's probably good they can't understand us for what we are.

Director: Why's that?

Lawyer: Because then their spirits would be crushed.

Director: Oh, you're not as awesome as all that. But you are impressive.

Lawyer: I suppose that's all we can ask. I really do want harmony with the plebs.

Director: Before or after you strike them with fear.

Lawyer: After. Fear is still necessary, I believe.

Director: And you strike fear by making examples.

Lawyer: Yes, all the big ones at once—to scare the hell out of them.

Director: What's wrong with constant little fears?

Lawyer: They have a corrosive effect. The great purge is good for health.

Director: And if there is sickness later? Another great purge?

Lawyer: We cut out the cancer. No more, no less.

Director: Doctors of the regime.

Lawyer: Yes! That's what we will be. Doctors of the regime. We work for its health.

Director: And if the aristocrats need doctoring? Who operates on them?

Lawyer: Doctor, heal thyself. And we will.

Director: What do you do? Take a vote on what's best? The majority rules? Or maybe some select plebs have a say here.

Lawyer: You must be kidding. What could they possibly contribute?

Director: Sometimes you need a fresh set of eyes.

Lawyer: Well, I know where we'll find those eyes. We'll find them in you.

103

Director: I can see helping certain individuals. But helping the body politic as a whole? I'm not sure what I can do.

Lawyer: Just come and describe what you see.

Director: That's it?

Lawyer: That's it. You might notice something we had overlooked—something that matters. We'll take it from there.

Director: Seeing what's wrong and taking care of what's wrong are two very different things.

Lawyer: I know there's no guarantee we'll correct what's wrong.

Director: What do you think might stop you?

Lawyer: Our old friend jealousy again.

Director: How might that get in the way?

Lawyer: You might say we should listen more to certain men on certain things. Jealousy might prevent us from doing this.

Director: And the same holds if I suggest they be given positions of command?

Lawyer: Of course.

Director: And I say certain people hold too much sway?

Lawyer: That's probably not so much a matter of jealously as an error of judgment on our part.

Director: Might it be a matter of wounded pride?

Lawyer: For both the ones who hold too much sway and those who allow them that, yes.

Director: You like to think your judgments on men are sound.

Lawyer: We do. And while they generally are, we're human and make mistakes.

Director: What if I find you've made lots of mistakes?

Lawyer: That's unlikely. But if you do, one of two things is possible. One, you're mistaken. Two, we've grown corrupt.

Director: I know how I might be mistaken. But how would you be corrupt?

Lawyer: We make decisions for the wrong reasons.

Director: Can you give an example?

Lawyer: We put someone in a particular role because his lineage seems best—not because he's best for the job.

Director: Why would you do that?

Lawyer: Because we want lineage to protect us.

Director: You use lineage as a crutch.

Lawyer: Yes, exactly. No aristocrat should ever use a crutch—except for a broken leg.

Director: Metaphorically speaking, what's a broken leg?

Lawyer: Well, a broken leg means you can't stand on your own. When can't an aristocrat stand on his own?

Director: When the money dries up from the plebs.

Lawyer: Their economy grows bad, yes.

Director: It's never good when aristocrats feel the pinch.

Lawyer: Oh, give us some credit. We'll simply retreat into virtuous austerity.

Director: And you'll think highly of yourselves for it?

Lawyer: Yes, we will. We'll be proud of our ability to adjust and cope. We'll work to rebuild the pleb economy. And we'll learn from our mistakes—whatever they might be.

Director: What if the economy went off the rails due to interference from a foreign power?

Lawyer: We'd go to war.

Director: A trade war?

Lawyer: Whatever kind of war it takes.

Director: I take it there will be conscription among the plebs.

Lawyer: Certainly.

Director: And they'll fight because they're protecting their own.

Lawyer: That's the best reason to fight.

Director: How will they know you have their best interests at heart?

Lawyer: Because we're part of the same body politic.

Director: You are the head, I suppose. And they are the heart.

Lawyer: No! We are both head and heart.

Director: What of the plebs?

Lawyer: They are the stomach. They are ruled by their appetites.

Director: And you are ruled by reason and your pride.

Lawyer: Precisely.

Director: If reason and pride conflict, what do you do?

Lawyer: We think again.

Director: You never sacrifice your pride?

Lawyer: Never.

Director: This might be a flaw that I'd point out when you're sick.

Lawyer: I'm not talking about being obstinate when you're wrong. I'm talking about a certain kind of self-love.

Director: So you're saying to love yourself always.

Lawyer: I am.

Director: Can't the plebs do that?

Lawyer: They can. But in an aristocrat—there's more to love.

104

Director: What do you love more? Your family or yourself?

Lawyer: My family is myself.

Director: You're not overly concerned with being an individual.

Lawyer: The individual is a democratic thing. Aristocrats are part of a whole. We're woven into the fabric of things.

Director: The whole, the fabric—this is the family.

Lawyer: Yes, and eventually all aristocrats are related.

Director: The ruling class is one big family unit.

Lawyer: And that's as it should be.

Director: And striving for excellence doesn't interfere?

Lawyer: Striving for excellence tightens the weave. Think of a sheet of the highest quality. It has thousands and thousands of threads woven tight as can be. That's a good aristocracy.

Director: And if one thread isn't pulled tight, things might unravel?

Lawyer: Yes. And that's why in an aristocracy we take great pains to ensure everyone is doing well.

Director: No doubt. So you're part of the fabric whether you like it or not.

Lawyer: Believe me—we like it.

Director: But if someone doesn't? Relocation?

Lawyer: But why wouldn't they like it? All the higher needs are met.

Director: Apparently not for some. So can they leave?

Lawyer: If we all left when the going got tough, where would we be?

Director: But 'we all' don't want to leave, perhaps especially when the going gets tough.

Lawyer: True. So maybe relocation is the thing. But it can't come easy.

Director: Why not? Are you afraid everyone will opt to leave?

Lawyer: Of course not.

Director: Then make relocation a simple and easy thing. It will speak well of you, you know. It shows you have great confidence in the quality of your regime.

Lawyer: That's true. Simple and easy it is. It has to be. Or what are we? But it's only allowed once you've become an adult.

Director: Of course. The storms of adolescence shouldn't lead to this.

Lawyer: But it will reflect badly on the family from which the relocated comes. They didn't handle those storms very well.

Director: Everyone knows certain people just don't fit in. Try as you might, there's nothing to be done but let them go.

Lawyer: Agreed.

Director: But the vast majority will fit, or else you're doing something wrong.

Lawyer: While it doesn't do to speak of 'vast' in an aristocracy, I take your point. Child rearing is the most important thing.

Director: What's the first thing you teach a child?

Lawyer: Security. The child must have confidence in his place in the world. It must be dyed in his wool.

Director: And then?

Lawyer: Gratitude for what he's got.

Director: Gratitude toward whom?

Lawyer: The family as a whole.

Director: So, ultimately, gratitude toward all other aristocrats.

Lawyer: Yes.

Director: What else?

Lawyer: Probity, of which we've noted the importance before.

Director: Probity toward aristocrats; probity toward the plebs.

Lawyer: Yes. We must teach our children that while the plebs are lower, they are an integral part of our regime. We must keep them healthy.

Director: When are the youths first exposed to the plebs?

Lawyer: I've changed my view on this. They are exposed right away in the hospital after birth. The nurses are plebs. The doctors are plebs. There are plebs all around.

Director: Of course. Do they ever encounter plebs of their own age?

Lawyer: Rarely.

Director: Not even through sporting events?

Lawyer: Especially not through sporting events. Think about it. If we win, that's only what we'd expect. But if we lose....

Director: Doesn't losing build character?

Lawyer: That's not the kind of character we want to build. The children must understand they are of a different class. For a class to work you need to build walls.

Director: We're so used to hearing that tearing down walls is good.

Lawyer: Some walls are bad; others are good.

Director: What's a bad wall?

Lawyer: One you hide behind.

Director: And a good wall?

Lawyer: A good wall allows things to grow within that couldn't grow without.

105

Director: Your children need to be walled in.

Lawyer: Now I don't like the metaphor. As I've said, the children are mingling with the plebs from the time they are born.

Director: How about with the rest of the outside world?

Lawyer: That's another matter. We wait until they're twenty-five for that.

Director: Why twenty-five?

Lawyer: That's when we're sure their character has set, when we're sure the character is proof against the outside world.

Director: What might happen if they go too young? Corruption?

Lawyer: Put simply, yes.

Director: Oh, I think you're worried about nothing. So what if they see a democracy? Will that make democrats of them?

Lawyer: It's not the democracies I worry about. It's the kingships or tyrannies or plutocracies.

Director: What is it with these regimes?

Lawyer: They can have all the trappings with none of the work.

Director: You honestly think your youth would be attracted to that? They would miss excellence like they'd miss an arm or a leg. No, they would have contempt for these regimes. Take them to them as early and often as you like. They'll only learn to appreciate more what they have. And they'll gain in knowledge of men.

Lawyer: Maybe I am too cautious here. I'll have to give it some thought.

Director: Good. And while we're at it, when will your children learn to fight?

Lawyer: From the earliest possible age. They'll learn all the martial arts. Physical cowardice brings moral cowardice.

Director: And the other way round?

Lawyer: Definitely.

Director: So you'll train them in moral courage?

Lawyer: Absolutely.

Director: How does one do that?

Lawyer: You put them in difficult situations and see what they do.

Director: And then you coach them?

Lawyer: Yes.

Director: Are you harsh when they fail the test?

Lawyer: We don't have to be. We just show a little disappointment and give some encouraging words.

Director: That's it?

Lawyer: You have to know the nature of these kids. They want nothing more than to please.

Director: Why do you think that is? Are kids everywhere eager to please?

Lawyer: You know how certain pure bred dogs have certain sorts of personalities? That's how it is with our kids. It's in their nature.

Director: And if it's not?

Lawyer: We'll always have exceptions to the rule.

Director: How will you work with them?

Lawyer: Through fear of relocation at age twenty-five.

Director: You'd let the bad apple stay that long in the bushel?

Lawyer: Relocation is serious, a permanent thing. We have to give them every chance.

Director: Will the other kids know this might happen?

Lawyer: Oh yes, certainly. From earliest youth they're told it's relocation for those who can't listen.

Director: And to put some teeth in it you actually have to relocate someone from time to time. What's the most terrible thing about relocation?

Lawyer: The family that's left behind.

Director: Do they mourn it as a death?

Lawyer: Yes. Or they celebrate it as a good riddance.

Director: Yes, that's a sort of terrible thing.

Lawyer: Either way, it makes a great impression on the young.

Director: Would you make relocation mandatory?

Lawyer: What do you mean?

Director: Each year the worst of the lot is sent away.

Lawyer: Oh, you mean it like those corporations that fire the bottom ten percent each year. No, we'd never do that.

Director: Why not?

Lawyer: We're a family, Director. We want everyone to stay. We only send someone packing if they force us to. We give them every chance.

Director: What if someone simply wants to leave? Free to go?

Lawyer: I don't know. I suppose they should be free. But once they go it's a permanent thing.

Director: Why no second chance?

Lawyer: Our youth need to expect a high level of stability in all things.

Director: To keep them grounded.

Lawyer: Yes. A relocation, or voluntary departure, is a traumatic thing for the community—regardless of whether it's best for all involved.

106

Director: The community must be one.

Lawyer: There must be oneness in us, yes.

Director: Why is oneness good?

Lawyer: If you don't know, I feel sorry for you. Oneness is like being wrapped in a warm blanket on a cold winter night.

Director: Oneness keeps you warm?

Lawyer: Yes, but that's not my point. There is no metaphysical unease when you are one with your community.

Director: And if there is you get transported.

Lawyer: If there is, there's something wrong—you're sick. You need medical help.

Director: Who can best provide this help?

Lawyer: It's hard to say. Usually it's someone the sick one has a natural attraction to. It could be a peer; it could be an elder.

Director: So what do they do?

Lawyer: They talk and talk until the root of the problem is clear.

Director: And then?

Lawyer: They take steps.

Director: That sounds ominous.

Lawyer: No, I didn't mean it that way. I mean we take steps towards one another.

Director: You meet them halfway?

Lawyer: As long as the way is good, we'd be willing to go more than halfway. We'd be willing to go all the way.

Director: The willingness shows your love.

Lawyer: Yes, exactly. The oneness of the community is love. This is our strength. We love the excellence in each other.

Director: You like belonging to something greater than yourself.

Lawyer: Doesn't everyone? It's just that our 'something' is the best something there is.

Director: And if you ever found a better something?

Lawyer: What better could there be?

Director: I don't know. I'm just wondering. Are you open to it?

Lawyer: I don't see how I could be.

Director: Why not?

Lawyer: Oneness and openness don't go hand in hand.

Director: Then you have a serious problem.

Lawyer: What problem?

Director: How will your people know—know—they have the best?

Lawyer: They'll feel it. And when they look around they'll see nothing better.

Director: How will they know nothing is better?

Lawyer: Nothing will appeal to them.

Director: What if something appeals to you?

Lawyer: Crisis. But it won't happen.

Director: How can you be so sure?

Lawyer: I know enough to appreciate what I have.

Director: Because you're one of the founders of the regime?

Lawyer: Yes.

Director: Don't you wish you could teach later generations what you know, what you appreciate?

Lawyer: We'll always teach about the founding. We'll teach our descendants what things were like.

Director: But can they ever really know?

Lawyer: No. And I suppose that's fine. Why have them know existential suffering?

Director: That's what democracy is to you?

Lawyer: And to you. This lowest common denominator stuff kills the soul. The higher soul. I'm heartily sick of it. I crave something more.

Director: But don't you have plenty of freedom?

Lawyer: Yes, but freedom to do what?

Director: Live your life.

Lawyer: The life I want to live involves being immersed in the few.

Director: So immerse yourself in them. Cut ties with your democratic friends. Aren't you at a stage in your career where you can be selective in who you represent?

Lawyer: Yes. But I want to rule.

Director: There's the trick. You want to rule. You can't be happy, or satisfied, unless you rule. You can't stand the thought of the democrats being above you. Not even in the tall tower in which you work do you feel removed from them. They're everywhere.

Lawyer: Yes, it's true.

Director: Well, I don't know what to tell you, other than what we've already said.

Lawyer: So I'm stuck hoping for some calamity to bring about my regime.

Director: It's an awful thing to hope for calamity.

Lawyer: It is. But, fortunately, things seem to be going my way.

107

Director: So what are you? A passive hopeful?

Lawyer: Would you rather I be an active conspirator?

Director: An active hopeful sounds good.

Lawyer: Tell me about active hope.

Director: You talk about your hopes.

Lawyer: In secret with friends.

Director: In public with all.

Lawyer: Ha! I'll be shouted down! And worse!

Director: You think you'll get death threats?

Lawyer: I know I will. Don't you know we're playing with fire?

Director: The we mustn't play. Do you know what kind of example of courage you could set for the cause?

Lawyer: Sure. But what about my wife and son?

Director: You think they're not strong?

Lawyer: It's not that. But I haven't talked to them about all this.

Director: Who have you spoken with about all this?

Lawyer: You.

Director: What? Not your aristocratically inclined friends?

Lawyer: We talk. But not in so much depth. You should come and speak to them.

Director: How many of them are there?

Lawyer: Three.

Director: So it's you four fingers and me, the thumb.

Lawyer: Would you?

Director: I would. I want to test their mettle to see if this talk is nothing but a dream. What positions do they hold?

Lawyer: One runs a private equity fund; one has his own company; and one is a political chief of staff.

Director: An interesting mix. But I'm wary of the last.

Lawyer: Why?

Director: He's at the heart of democratic politics.

Lawyer: Yes, but he's looking for a change. He's grown to hate politics as we know it.

Director: Then why hasn't he gotten out?

Lawyer: He's working on that. But where to go? What should he be? A political consultant? Same problem, different role. Or maybe he could be an officer at a large corporation? A corporate tool? No thanks, He's looking for fundamental change. And aristocracy is it.

Director: Why does the one with his own company want aristocracy? Not so successful in democratic times?

Lawyer: No, he's very successful. But in the process of taking his company public he's learned some bad things about the democratic economy.

Director: The economy is democratic?

Lawyer: It's the hypocrisy that kills him. The people who run it pretend to be democrats.

Director: What are they?

Lawyer: Oligarchs, plutocrats. He wants nothing to do with that.

Director: And what about the private equity man? Isn't private equity isolated from democracy?

Lawyer: It is. And he wants more of the isolation.

Director: Well, it sounds like you have some interesting friends. I'd like to meet them. But how do we stop from conspiring for the overthrow of the duly constituted government?

Lawyer: It's no crime to talk. We simply take no steps.

Director: We let others take the steps for us?

Lawyer: Here we are, passive again. What can we do?

Director: Take no steps but prepare the ground for when and if it's needed.

Lawyer: We always need ground.

Director: Yes, but we must sweep it for landmines first.

Lawyer: Who would plant these mines? The democrats?

Director: The worst of their kind.

Lawyer: Why are they the worst? They're just protecting their kind.

Director: Landmines create a sort of moat around a castle.

Lawyer: Democrats live in a caste?

Director: The oligarchs who call themselves democrats do. That's where the danger lies. The people are more open to reason than we think.

Lawyer: You surprise me.

Director: That's because I'm telling it like it is.

108

Lawyer: How do you know the people are open to reason?

Director: Because when you talk about something that touches their interests, they listen.

Lawyer: Yes, but their interests are very narrow.

Director: And the interests of aristocrats are broad?

Lawyer: As broad as can be.

Director: Why?

Lawyer: Because aristocrats are not on the make.

Director: Yes, but they're ambitious. And sometimes the object of their ambition is more narrow than the interests of the plebs. How do we prevent this?

Lawyer: Prevent narrow ambitions? We teach our young that narrowness is base. An aristocrat takes the broad view. Narrowness is the result of a cramped way of thinking.

Director: What cramps a pleb?

Lawyer: The harsh necessity to earn a living.

Director: So there's no excuse for an aristocrat.

Lawyer: None. We must tame the narrow ambition in the soul.

Director: Can tame ambition ever be great?

Lawyer: We should harness not tame.

Director: How do we harness our ambition?

Lawyer: We attach it to the welfare of the community.

Director: Unharnessed ambition can tear the world apart.

Lawyer: Yes, it can—and often does.

Director: So it's love for one's own against love for one's glory.

Lawyer: That puts it well.

Director: But do you want to disparage glory? Glory for excellent things?

Lawyer: We don't want glory. We want appreciation.

Director: And that's enough?

Lawyer: If you truly had peers who were your more or less equals, appreciation would be more than enough.

Director: So there's a range of equality.

Lawyer: No doubt. Some are better at one thing; some are better at another.

Director: And some are not so good at anything at all.

Lawyer: True. But they can be good in acknowledging others. The least of the family is family still. They are loved for their lack of envy.

Director: Will the plebs always envy?

Lawyer: The best of them will admire.

Director: And what's their reward?

Lawyer: To have something to admire.

Director: I think you should invite these people to certain ceremonies.

Lawyer: What ceremonies?

Director: Oh, I don't know. Rites of coming of age?

Lawyer: Director, that's a very private family affair. Why would we want outsiders there?

Director: Because you can show them that while they aren't family, they are honored friends. You can build great good will this way—good will that helps anchor your regime.

Lawyer: Well, you do have a point.

Director: Allow a little breath of fresh air. Besides, the contrast with the plebs will make the aristocrats present feel that much more grand.

Lawyer: Alright, you've made your point.

Director: Ceremonies will play a great part among the few.

Lawyer: I agree. But why are you so sure?

Director: Excellence needs recognition. What better way than through ceremonies.

Lawyer: You're right. What pleasure they'll give—so long as jealousy doesn't set in.

Director: What can be done about that?

Lawyer: Well, we're not going to distribute feel good awards to all who are present. I will not cheapen excellence this way.

Director: So what's to be done?

Lawyer: People must be glad for the excellent, the way brother would for brother.

Director: Sibling rivalry is the worst. How do parents stop that?

Lawyer: The best they can do is turn it into healthy competition.

Director: How?

Lawyer: You find what each is good at, then you encourage them in that.

Director: And praise them equally?

Lawyer: If both are trying? Yes.

Director: So if one is good at war, and is good with books—equals?

Lawyer: They have to be in order to keep the family intact. And maybe the one good in books can write about war.

Director: And maybe the one good in war can enter the lists in the war of books.

Lawyer: Sure, that would be good. But what do you mean about the war of books?

Director: Polemics. Books meant to stir. In fact, speeches can be polemics. You might give a speech acknowledged as a polemic about the virtues of aristocracy.

Lawyer: Yes, but I don't have a brother in war to back me up.

Director: You only have me.

109

Lawyer: You'd really back me up in a speech about aristocracy? In today's climate?

Director: I really would. But I'd be honest, you know.

Lawyer: What do you mean?

Director: I'd say your linchpin concept of excellence is vague.

Lawyer: How is it vague? We know it when we see it.

Director: That's how it's vague.

Lawyer: How would you make it more concrete?

Director: I'd tie it more to the welfare of the plebs. We are talking about excellence in rule above all else, yes?

Lawyer: Yes, of course.

Director: Well, who is most ruled but the plebs? We have to see they're doing well.

Lawyer: We'll know it when we see it?

Director: I was thinking we'd borrow tools from democracy.

Lawyer: What, polls?

Director: And other ways of gathering data. Do you object?

Lawyer: Of course I do! We're not going to become the servants of the plebs.

Director: You hardly would be their servants. How do you expect to know how you're doing?

Lawyer: We'd take their temperature by talking to them.

Director: And do you think they'd speak freely?

Lawyer: I would hope they wouldn't! A certain amount of deference is due.

Director: And if the deference frays, you know something is amiss.

Lawyer: Precisely. If there's fraying of manners, we'll look into it more.

Director: You'll find out the cause

Lawyer: Right. And then we remedy it.

Director: And when you have, the plebs' manners will be perfectly good, which is to say perfectly submissive.

Lawyer: Deferential, not submissive. A pleb is not a slave.

Director: Are you sure you wouldn't have slaves if you could?

Lawyer: Yes.

Director: Why not?

Lawyer: Slaves bring you down. If you debase a human being, you in turn are debased.

Director: The plebs aren't debased?

Lawyer: No, they're not. Just because they don't rule doesn't mean they're debased.

Director: But they're not free.

Lawyer: Neither are the few!

Director: There is no freedom in your realm.

Lawyer: Freedom is overrated—and usually a lie.

Director: I'd like to see you say that to democrats today.

Lawyer: Why, so I'd have to dodge rocks thrown at me?

Director: Because I think you might find more than one who agrees.

Lawyer: Yes, but their answer is to fight for freedom. Mine is to replace freedom with duty and all it entails.

Director: That might be attractive to some.

Lawyer: Why don't you get up and say these things?

Director: Because I'm not a proponent of aristocracy.

Lawyer: Why not?

Director: I don't believe in it the way you do.

Lawyer: You don't think it will bring excellence?

Director: Vague though that might be, I think some excellence will be had.

Lawyer: But not enough.

Director: It remains to be seen.

Lawyer: Though not a proponent, you're not opposed?

Director: I'm not opposed to talking about it. In fact, I'm in favor of talking about it. But I can't say if I'm opposed or not unless I see how things take shape.

Lawyer: Do you prefer democracy?

Director: I prefer whatever regime makes sense, given the times.

Lawyer: So you're a trimmer?

Director: Do I trim my sails to suit the wind? That seems fair. But I wouldn't say I'm blown with the wind. I tack very hard to say on course.

Lawyer: Where do you want to go?

Director: Wherever philosophy takes me.

Lawyer: Where does philosophy take you now?

Director: To an excellent feast with an excellent, victorious friend.

Lawyer: Yes, yes. But whereto?

Director: Toward uncharted lands.

Lawyer: Aristocracy has been charted many times before.

Director: But it's a whole new continent here.

Printed in the United States
by Baker & Taylor Publisher Services